GHOSTS

WASHINGTON'S MOST FAMOUS GHOST STORIES

BY JOHN ALEXANDER

WBT

Book Design by: Ed Schneider
Cover Design by: Terry Dale
Photo Editor: Lynn Buchheit

Published by The Washington Book Trading Company
P.O. Box 1676, Arlington, Virginia 22210

Copyright 1988 by The Washington Book Trading Company
Illustrations Copyright 1988 by
The Washington Book Trading Company

Library of Congress Catalog number 75-27691
ISBN number 0-915168-07-3 (paper)

Picture Credits

*In the Washington you are about to dis-
cover, past, present, and future are sometimes intertwined. You will wander in and
out of two centuries of history along with
the ghosts of Washington who, from time
to time, are said to revisit their beloved
city.*

CONTENTS

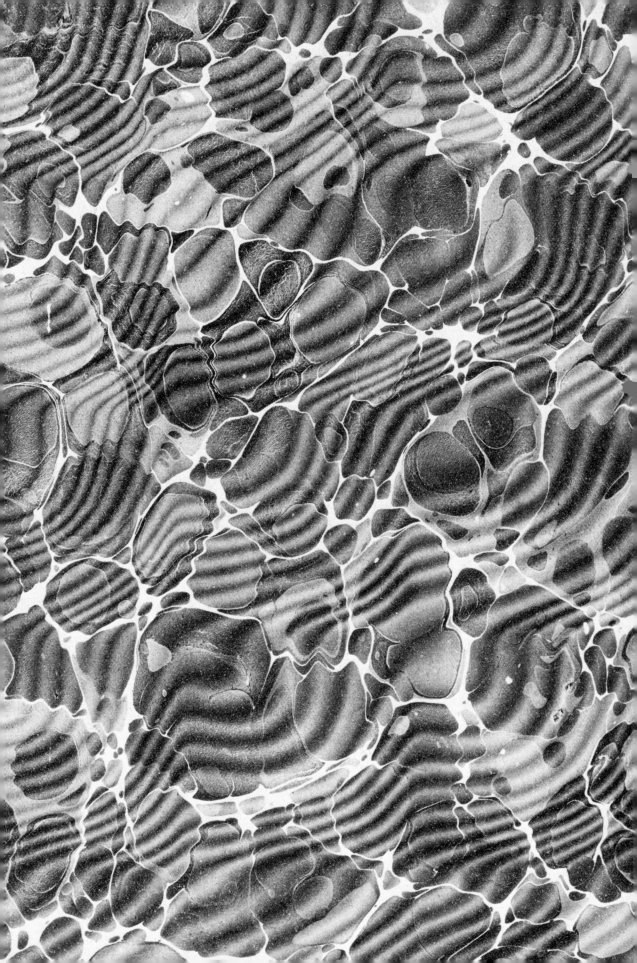

INTRODUCTION

This book grew out of an hour-long radio special I put together for WMAL Radio in Washington for Halloween of 1970. "Washington Revisited," as it was called, was an abbreviated supernatural tour of Halcyon House, the Capitol, Commodore Stephen Decatur's home, and the White House. It received such a gratifying response, including an Ohio State Journalism Award, that the station has continued to air it every Halloween since, and I have continued to collect new tales and additional details about the old ones.

The stories I have gathered are deeply embedded in the folklore and history of our Nation's Capital. Most of the names and quite a few of the buildings mentioned in these encounters with the spirit world will be familiar to you.

Down through the years there have been a variety of explanations of how the tales originated. Some have been attributed to too much drink or a too fertile imagination. Some reported experiences have been written off as fantasies inspired by the workings of the subconscious. But there are those who argue that supernatural occurrences are exactly what they

appear to be: meetings with spirits that have transcended the grave.

It is not necessarily the explanation of how a tale may have originated that I am concerned with, though, but rather its preservation. Some ghost stories came down through the years by word of mouth, as they were told and retold by people who became personally involved in a part of the city's history that fascinated them. Certain encounters made such an impression on friends and neighbors of the person who first told about it that the story survived with little or no mention in the press. A surprising number of the stories, however, also found their way into newspapers of the day. Had they not appeared in print, there is a pretty good chance that most of them would have been lost, for many aren't told as often as they once were, and some incidents that I found in yellowed newspapers of a century or so ago aren't remembered at all—even in the neighborhoods where they originated.

It was the senior citizens of the neighborhoods I visited who were the most helpful in recalling the old tales, but I found a surprising interest in ghost lore

2 among some younger District residents too. More and more of them seem to be curious about the history of the particular house or area where they have settled.

Today, most unexplainable parapsychological phenomena go unreported in newspapers and periodicals. Although the nomenclature might have changed, the nature of the experiences hasn't, yet journalists claim either that such occurrences have become too frequent to report or that they are just too difficult to document.

Yesterday's ghost story may have been replaced by today's parapsychological happening, but in most instances we are no closer to answers than we were 125 years ago when great numbers of Americans first began their romance with ghosts. It was in the 1850's that spiritualism began to sweep the nation, and attempts to communicate with the dead became a popular pastime. Newspaper reporters often chronicled the exploits of mediums and devoted column upon column to meetings with spirits and tales of houses visited by "departed souls."

During the 1920's and 30's, new supernatural encounters were reported less frequently, and articles from that period on seemed for the most part to retell the older stories, but they were growing less interesting and lacked detail. Along with the nation's preoccupation with science in the 1950's came a much harder approach to ghost stories. Reporters began to investigate more closely and to seek verification from several sources. As a result, many of the stories fell by the wayside for lack of proof.

Many of the older dwellings and public buildings in the Federal City are full of supernatural lore, but not every building in Washington is haunted. For instance, you would think that either Abraham Lincoln or John Wilkes Booth would haunt Ford's Theatre, or that Lincoln would visit the Petersen house where he died, but I found no such stories. Abe apparently prefers the White House, where scores of people in every administration since Grant's have reported his presence. Blair House, the Frederick Douglass

House, the original Smithsonian Institution buildings, and many more—seem to meet the requirements, but I could uncover no stories about ghosts having been seen in any of them.

Quite a few of the houses that do have ghosts, have been haunted for so long that the spirits who return to them have practically become members of the family. Indeed, who's to say they weren't at one time? Sometimes, however, it is impossible to pinpoint the exact location of a house that has a supernatural story connected with it. In the retelling of tales the facts about where the house is can become distorted. In some cases wary inhabitants are reluctant to discuss their nocturnal visitors at all, or if they do talk to reporters, they ask to have the address omitted from the story. They are understandably apprehensive that neighbors might ridicule them if their secret gets out, or that they will be invaded by tourists. A few have even expressed concern over what the visitors from the spirit world might do to them or to the house if they are angered.

The tales you will read on these pages are considerably different from those in Hans Holzer's 1971 book, *The Ghosts that Walk in Washington*. Holzer began by talking about the "ill-fated Kennedys" and listed accounts of psychics who had tried to warn the family of impending tragedy. Then, accompanied by a medium, Holzer went to Northern Virginia and to a home near Baltimore to exorcise a few ghosts. But other than accounts of his visits to check out the existence of spirits at the Octagon and the Woodrow Wilson house, the reader will find little about the famous ghosts of the District of Columbia. Most of those are dismissed with little more than a paragraph in the final chapter. That is where this book begins.

A special thanks to my professional colleagues of the past, and to a score of curators, Columbia Historical Society personnel, to those who work in the Washingtoniana section of the Martin Luther King Jr. Library, and to WMAL Radio where I told my first ghost story.

J.A.
August 20, 1975
Washington, D.C.

GEORGE TOWN

Rock Creek

PART of VIRGINIA within the TERRITORY of COLUMBIA

POTOMACK RIVER

President House

PLAN
of the CITY of
WASHINGTON

Statute Miles
1/4   1/2   1

A 1798 plan for the city of Washington.

Published by J. Stockdale.

Tiber Creek

Capitol

Capitol Street

Carolina

East

North

Carolina

Kentucky

South

Georgia

EASTERN BRANCH

PART of MARYLAND within the TERRITORY of COLUMBIA

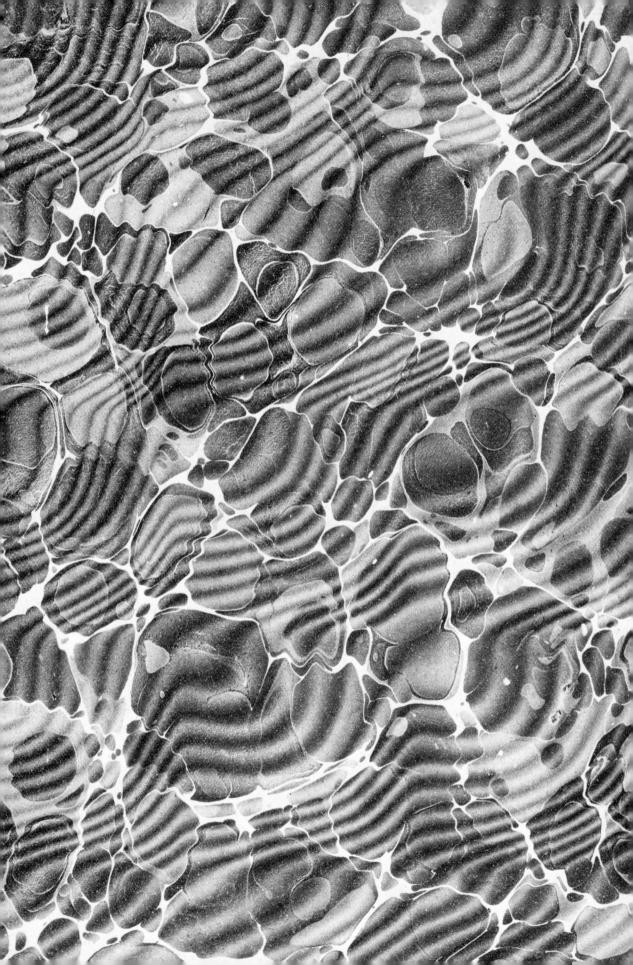

1. GEORGE-TOWN

THE CURSE OF THE THREE SISTERS

As you leave the Capital Beltway and drive along the scenic George Washington Parkway on the Virginia side of the Potomac, you are on land that was once part of the mighty Powhatan Confederacy. Between the Chain Bridge and Key Bridge, three large granite rocks rise out of the river. They are part of a legendary Indian curse that persists to this day that no one will cross the river at this point.

Scores of people who have tried to cross the river here have died in the attempt. Almost four hundred years ago Captain John Smith wrote in his diary about the sounds of moaning and sobbing coming from the vicinity of the Three Sisters Rocks, and referred to the curse. Some say it is the curse of the three sisters that has thwarted the efforts of those who have wanted to erect a massive span between Chain Bridge and Key Bridge where the three rocks break the surface of the Potomac. The bridge was begun and steel pilings appeared briefly near the District of Columbia

shore, directly on the other side of the midchannel rocks. It has yet to be built.

To understand why the Three Sisters Rocks and the curse that surrounds them command such respect from many Washingtonians, it is necessary to go back to almost a full century before the Europeans settled Jamestown in 1607.

Indian enclaves and confederacies dotted the fertile region west of the Chesapeake Bay and on either side of the mighty Potomac River. Tribal medicine men were important leaders because of the powerful magic they received directly from the Great Spirit. Our story involves three daughters of one such spiritual leader.

From the settlements along the river, the Indians launched their hunting trips and their war parties. The region was rich in resources. In addition to the seasonal fish runs, game, wild berries, nuts, and seeds abounded in the woodlands. The Indians here also grew their own maize, beans, and squash.

Although the twenty thousand or so Indians living in the region were Al-

The Three Sisters Rocks—those small islands in the Potomac—are mute reminders of the curse that has plagued this section of the river for four hundred years.

gonquian and spoke similar languages, there was quite a bit of animosity between the groups that lived in what is now Maryland and those that settled along the Potomac in what is now Northern Virginia. Northern Indians of Iroquoian stock, and the Susquehannocks, often made raids into the area of the Powhatan Confederacy (composed of several Algonquian tribes). The warfare was frequent and ruthless. Control of the entire region's abundant resources was the prize for the victor. Battle captives were almost always tortured, sometimes enslaved, and infrequently adopted.

One day, after what had been a particularly long siege, the chief of a Virginia village decided that the situation had stabilized enough so that he could take his men out in search of venison and other game. Food supplies in the palisaded village were depleted. The warriors had fought many days to break the siege and drive the Susquehannock raiders back across the river. Hunger had weakened them, and their survival hinged on that one last desperate effort to end the siege. Starvation had already claimed a few old men and women who had sacrificed their rations so that the warriors and the young might live. When the chief decided he and his men could undertake the hunt, he refused to give three of his young sons permission to come along. He thought they weren't old enough to defend themselves if the hunters encountered their enemy outside the village.

The sons were greatly disappointed. Eager to prove their bravery—and impress their father—they devised a plan. They would launch a clandestine expedition to bring back a catch of enough fresh fish to feed the women, children, and old men until the hunting party returned.

The greatest abundance of fish was near the northern shore, and although the young men knew how dangerous it would be to venture there, that did not affect their determination to prove their manhood to their father. All but one of the village canoes had been ripped to shreds by the Susquehannocks. The chief's sons had hidden it, and as dawn drew near, they slipped the canoe from its hiding place and quietly paddled across the river before the sun could burn away the early morning fog.

Unfortunately, the Susquehannocks had left behind a scouting party. The three brothers were fishing only a short while when they were attacked. In full view of those who had remained in the village across the river, the chief's sons were tortured and scalped.

Among the villagers who watched helplessly were the medicine man's three beautiful daughters, who were deeply in love with the unfortunate braves. Although numb with shock and disbelief, the maidens called upon all their inner strength to seek revenge. They decided to cross the river and persuade the rival chief to give them to the warriors who had slain their lovers. The maidens envisioned a slow, torturous death for these hated enemies once they had them in the power of their beauty and their father's medicine.

Tears streamed down their faces as they lashed several logs together to improvise a makeshift raft. Wading into the water, they climbed onto the logs and shoved off from the shore. None of the other villagers noticed that they were gone until it was too late.

The river proved too swift. The winds were too strong. Currents began carrying the raft downstream toward the open sea. Stricken by the tragedy they had just witnessed and frustrated by their inability to navigate the Potomac, the maidens' sad faces glistened with their tears. They looked deep into one another's eyes and seemed to draw supernatural strength from each other. They clasped their arms around each other and shouted a curse. If they—the privileged daughters of the medicine man of the most powerful confederacy on earth—could not cross the river, then no one would cross at that point again. *Ever.*

The three sisters sealed the curse by jumping into the swiftly flowing waters, and, through death, rejoined their young braves.

The sky darkened as the young women sank from sight. Distant rumblings of thunder moved closer and closer. Lightning danced overhead. Occasionally bolts darted down to earth and touched the waters where the maidens had perished. The storm continued through the night, swelling the waters and whipping them into a white-capped frenzy.

At sunrise the waters subsided. A calm spread over the surface. As the clouds rolled away, the sun reflected brilliantly off the sparkling water, and off three granite boulders that had not been there the day before.

To this day the three rocks continue to take their toll of those who dare to defy the maidens' curse. Metropolitan Harbor Police add at least a half-dozen new names to the list of victims each year. Among these are swimmers, fishermen, and canoeists who try to cross the river at this point. Old rivermen say that a mournful cry heard drifting over the Potomac during a storm means there will soon be another drowning—another unsuspecting victim of the ancient curse of the three sisters.

As the controversy over construction of the Three Sisters Bridge reached its peak in 1972—with environmentalists opposing it—those who knew the legend saw a strange, historic parallel in a storm that descended at a crucial juncture, just as it had when the three Indian maidens had invoked their curse. The skies over Washington darkened, distant rumblings of thunder moved closer, winds churned the mighty Potomac into a white frenzy. Lightning flashed overhead, and it is said that bolts darted down to earth and touched the waters. Flood waters from the most devastating storm in the city's history swept away the construction framework at the proposed site for the Three Sisters Bridge. More than one bridge worker considered this mute testimony to the power of the ancient curse.

All hope of building the bridge seems to have been abandoned. Even plans to name the span for the three sisters seems to have failed to break the spell they cast over that section of the river.

The white men will never be alone.
These shores will swarm with the invisible dead.
The dead are not powerless.
Dead, did I say?
There is no death, only a change of worlds.

—WORDS OF A LONG-DEPARTED INDIAN CHIEF

The sound of British General Edward Braddock and his troops marching off to meet their death during the French and Indian War is still heard in the streets of Georgetown.

BRADDOCK'S DEATH MARCH

As you cross the Potomac from Virginia into Washington over Key Bridge, you see the pre-Revolutionary War port of Georgetown on the high ground directly ahead. The port is built on the ruins of what was once the Indian village of Tohoga. When the hour is late, the hillside rising out of the waters is said to echo with the sounds of soldiers on the march—soldiers from another time, killed at another place, yet inextricably involved in the old port's history.

The Europeans were determined to settle the region after the glowing reports sent back by Captain John Smith, who had sailed his ship up the Potomac. Henry Fleet, another Englishman, couldn't get Smith's description out of his mind. Within a few years after he read the Captain's diary, Fleet made plans to see the region for himself. What could a land be like that had "waters so clear the bottom could be seen to a depth of several fathoms"—as Smith described the Potomac? Fleet found out. He anchored his ship in the channel near Tohoga and spent some twelve years with the Indians.

Other Europeans followed to see for themselves this land that was so rich and fertile. The Indians were pushed farther back into the wilderness. As they became disgruntled, they found what they mistakenly thought was an ally in the French.

It was during the French and Indian War that Georgetown's most famous legend was born. General Edward Braddock had been brought to the Colonies in 1755 to fight the French after sensational victories in Holland. He would never return home. The optimistic Braddock landed his fourteen hundred troops in Alexandria, where they linked up with seven hundred Colonial militiamen and marched to the Georgetown Ferry. From there he sent half the men along the Potomac on the Virginia side, and personally led about one thousand troops across the river and up the hill through Georgetown. He planned to join the forces again in Cumberland, Maryland, where they would cross the Allegheny Mountains and attack the French at Fort Duquesne. He would make short work of these enemies of the Crown, Braddock thought.

However, at the Forks of the Ohio River, a combined French and Indian force one-third the size of Braddock's surprised him and his men. In the ensuing bloodbath Braddock and more than seven hundred of his men met their death.

On the bluffs above the Potomac where Braddock began his death march, more than one Georgetowner has reported hearing harshly barked orders, the rattling of sabers, and the clatter of horses' hoofs and men's boots on the old cobblestones. Those sounds of the distant past have shattered the stillness of Georgetown for more than two centuries—always on the anniversary of the start of Braddock's march.

A Civil War era journalist wrote an article for one of the Washington papers about a Union patrol's encounter with what might have been General Edward Braddock's doomed troops from the French and Indian War a hundred years earlier.

The writer says sentries for a Union force encamped on the District banks of the Potomac River heard the sounds of troops and equipment moving across Long Bridge. It was too dark to see anything, but troops quietly moved into battle position. When his men were set, the officer in charge sent a small patrol to scout the Rebs' position and strength.

The patrol came back wet to the skin and totally mystified. When they had heard what they thought was the advancing Rebel force, they had jumped over the side of Long Bridge to keep the enemy from spotting them. After the sounds had faded away, the patrol rushed back fully expecting to have been cut off behind their own lines.

The reporter said it was as if the Confederate troops had vanished in the middle of the bridge, but he speculated that it could have been the spirits of soldiers of another war that the Union patrol thought it heard.

Although the tale of Braddock's march continues to be told, and accounts of those who say they have witnessed it appear sporadically in some of the old Georgetown newspapers, I could find no one who would admit to personally having heard the invisible troops, who, according to legend, are doomed to march that road toward death throughout eternity.

MYSTERIOUS HAPPENINGS AT HALCYON HOUSE

Among the survivors of the Braddock massacre was a young lieutenant colonel of the Virginia militia—George Washington. He learned well from early defeats, and when the time came for him to assume a leadership role, he did not fail.

After the war, the new nation was in need of a Federal City, but the controversy over where to build it lasted longer than had the fight for freedom. From its

The spirit of Benjamin Stoddert, first Secretary of the Navy, has been seen over the years in his Georgetown house.

Stoddert's home—or what is left of it—still stands on a Georgetown bluff. Located on what is now Prospect Avenue, Northwest, Halcyon House, as Stoddert named it, bears little resemblance to the beautiful and smaller home he had erected on that site. Perhaps that is part of the explanation for all the mysterious occurrences that have been reported inside the turbulent old house: rapping and tapping sounds, an "unfamiliar figure" that sometimes appears, and other supernatural happenings.

Halcyon House—named for the mythical bird whose presence is said to calm the seas—has been anything but calm since the death of Stoddert. He had been a wealthy man and a friend to many of the nation's great leaders, including President Washington.

As a man who made his living from the sea, it seemed natural that Stoddert would want his home as near to it as possible. The land he chose sloped gently down to the Potomac. He commissioned the noted French planner Pierre Charles L'Enfant to design a magnificently terraced garden that enhanced the Potomac view. It also gave Stoddert a vantage point from which he could watch the merchant ships and frigates come and go with the winds. He must have felt mixed emotions as he gazed on such a placid scene, because most of the time that Stoddert served as Secretary of the Navy, his frigates were involved in an entanglement with the French that was anything but placid. In spite of this undeclared and minor sea war, Stoddert managed to get quite a bit accomplished in his government post. A tribute to his tireless energies was the expansion of the fleet and acquisition of land to construct navy yards for building more ships. It was also Stoddert who was responsible for organizing the Marine Corps on its present basis.

Stoddert was not quite so successful, however, at maintaining his personal affairs. When he stepped down as Secretary of the Navy at the end of John Adams's administration, Stoddert's shipping business was in such bad shape he simply couldn't pull it out. Within twelve years Benjamin Stoddert died, a frustrated and destitute man.

temporary home in Philadelphia, Congress ended the seven-year issue by selecting a one-hundred-square-mile tract on the banks of the Potomac. The location was chosen because it was halfway between New Hampshire—then the northernmost state, and Georgia—then the southernmost state.

Early attempts to make a city out of the District of Columbia—as the federal project had been named—met with something less than success. It seemed foolish to live anywhere but in the established port towns of Georgetown and Alexandria (Alexandria was ceded back to Virginia in 1846), when the rest of the area was largely meadows and mosquito-infested marshland.

The man President George Washington commissioned to purchase tracts of land for the District had a home in Georgetown. Benjamin Stoddert, a former Revolutionary War cavalry officer, also conducted his shipping business from there, except for one period of a few years when he served as the first Secretary of the United States Navy.

A rear view of Halcyon House as it looked before eccentric Albert Clemons went to work on it.

Several families passed through Halcyon House over the next few years. During the years preceding the Civil War—and possibly during the war too—it may have served as a crucial link in the Underground Railroad. An old Georgetown carpenter told me about runaway slaves, heading northward to freedom, who tried desperately to swim the Potomac and make it to a tunnel at river's edge that would take them to the basement of Halcyon House. Some drowned, but many survived the swim and were quartered in the cellar until they could regain the strength to continue on their road to freedom. The old carpenter also said that quite a few died in the basement of Halcyon House. The river proved too wide, their health too poor, and the cellar too damp for the weaker ones to recover.

"I have heard their cries, heard them plain as day," he said as his voice grew softer and his eyes took on a distant, glassy stare. The carpenter told me that when he was a young man, sometime around the turn of this century, he had been requested to wall up a tunnel in the cellar of Halcyon House. The family was having trouble with rats and was afraid they would find a way to the upstairs. The carpenter related how he took his lumber, nails, mortar, and several lanterns into the cellar one day to begin his task.

Back then, he had never heard any of the stories about the Underground Railroad or dying slaves. All he knew was that there were rats down there and he was scared. It was not the rats, however, that drove him from the cellar before he had completed plastering the wooden barricade that would forever seal the old tunnel. At first the carpenter thought he heard wind blowing through the tunnel. But the original low moan became a sob, another moan joined it, and then there was more sobbing.

He worked quickly, trying to concentrate on what he was doing and to convince himself it was only the wind, or maybe someone sick upstairs.

But just as he had plastered up most of the new wall, there was a blood-chilling scream, followed by the kind of sobbing only heard beside a deathbed. A gust of wind, which could not have come from the boarded-up tunnel, blew out his lanterns. The carpenter fled the cellar, never returning to pick up his tools. He could not get the sounds out of his mind, so he began asking questions about the history of the old house. He learned more than enough to convince him that those few hours he had spent in that cold, dank cellar were a visit into an unearthly world.

"Sometimes," he told me, "I wake up screaming in the middle of the night. My sweat's cold. It's been fifty to sixty years since I heard them sounds, and I'm still haunted by 'em. Haunted by my own mind trying to put faces to them poor people." He shook his head as though trying to clear his mind of the unpleasantness, "Guess I'll carry those ghostly cries to my grave." He did. A few months after I talked with him, the old Georgetown carpenter died.

His walling up of that old tunnel may have stopped the rats, but when the night is quiet and the hour is late, the moans, sobs, and cries of despair of which he spoke have continued to haunt residents and visitors.

As I searched the old and yellowed newspapers, I found a particular Georgetown house where recurring supernatural events were reported. It was described variously as a "house overlooking the river from the bluffs of Georgetown" or "overhanging M Street" or an "old sea captain's home," but most accounts contained enough other information to lead to the conclusion that all these writers were talking about Halcyon House. It was in the late 1800's that these unexplainable happenings began to attract the attention of reporters, and still no one has provided satisfactory answers to what causes them.

In the early decades of this century the wife of a retired Marine Corps major who lived in Halycon House had a startling experience. The newspaper account I read says she encountered a "woman dressed in costume of a forgotten period" while walking through a darkened hall one evening. The article also mentioned a history of "murmurs from servants" who "complained of weird noises during the night, and seeing strange shapes in rooms." The writer says the couple finally moved.

In the early 1930's a widow who owned the house kept quiet as long as she could and then finally told her story to a reporter just before she died. She described frequent tapping and rapping on the wall like that made by a heavy branch brushing it; yet, the reporter said, there were no trees nearby. The story also included accounts of servants who had met with a "strange person on the stairway who immediately disappeared." The widow told the reporter that for years she had pretended not to hear "muffled footsteps or the sounds of slippered feet," and would never discuss it. The widow suspected that Stoddert, who had died despondent, sick, and a virtual pauper, still walked through his home. The reporter recalled how "he just sat and waited for the day death would call him away from his invalid existence. . . . He used to sit by the window of his upstairs bedroom, with old-fashioned spy glass in hand, watching the harbor, watching the wharf . . . and watching the people."

After the widow died, the house remained vacant for a year or so before an eccentric named Albert Adsit Clemons acquired the property. He was not satisfied with the appearance of Stoddert's brick home, and set about to change it. Some think he just needed more room for his collection of religious paraphernalia, others think he began to collect it only after an encounter with Stoddert's ghost put the fear of God into him. One person who has done considerable research into Clemons's life told me the old man was fascinated by all forms of religion, and was particularly in awe of some Eastern philosophies. He is said to have embraced a belief that as long as he continued to build onto his earthly home, he would not die. Perhaps that is why Clemons pursued his construction with missionary zeal. He wrapped the north side of the house in a façade, four stories tall. Then he set about building apartments between the façade and Stoddert's original house.

The fear of death was deeply rooted in Clemons. He is said to have taken time out from building to ceremoniously bury

The rear of the house became the front when Clemons erected this façade as part of his never-ending building project, which he thought would give him ever-lasting life. His ghost is said to haunt the house, often manifesting its presence by turning off the electric lights that he would have no part of in life.

Albert Clemons used to shield the statues of angels that adorned Halcyon House by placing pie tins on their heads.

two mummies in the garden. One represented his lost figure; the other his lost youth. In the old coach house he constructed an apartment that contained a crypt in the middle of the floor. Some say he sometimes slept in it, but no one seems to know for whom he intended it, since he did not plan to die. Others think that possibly it was used as some sort of altar. Clemons liked stained glass, and Halcyon House was full of it. Some shattered multicolored evidence was still on the floor in the highest of three attics when I toured the old house. Like the stained glass on the floor, the beams in that third level attic came from St. Matthews Church on Rhode Island Avenue.

A researcher at the University of Maryland said he understood that Clemons obtained a cast-off pulpit when the old sanctuary at St. Matthews was razed. There is a platform in that third level loft and a high ceiling that could have accommodated the pulpit. The researcher said that some former tenants told him

that Clemons also had a giant crucifix carved from a tree up there. It was outside this attic, on the ledge overlooking Prospect Avenue, that Clemons had placed several statues of angels. He is said to have placed pie tins on the angels' heads to protect them when it rained. Another person with whom I spoke said that Clemons while vacationing in Italy supposedly had purchased an old church and had its contents shipped back to Halcyon House.

The eccentric's obsession that continuing construction meant continuing life drove him to persuade a carpenter to move in with him. Diligently they set to work. It is charged by some old Georgetowners that Clemons and his helper built with used lumber often salvaged from homes being demolished, and that their workmanship was shoddy.

Seldom did Clemons or the carpenter paint anything, let alone take time to draw up plans before reaching for the nails and hammer. The fever that infested Clemons compelled him to build without rhyme or reason. The inside of the house soon looked like a crazy quilt: some rooms were built without walls, there were doors that opened into blank walls, one stairway led nowhere. It had been covered over to become a closet. When Stoddert owned the home, the main staircase rose from the garden side of the house, but Clemons reversed it to the Prospect Avenue side. Clemons also joined the old coach house to the main building. It was said that the only criticism the carpenter ever had of his boss was that Clemons seldom knew what he wanted done, and that the carpenter often would spend a whole day tearing down much of the previous day's work because Clemons had changed his mind.

One of Clemons's pet projects was the ten apartments he helped to build inside the façade, which extended out from the main part of Halcyon House by twenty feet. To help finance his work, he then rented them out. He posted a sign on a lamppost out on the sidewalk that read:

Apartments for rent.
No Children.
No Dogs.
No leases.
No electricity permitted.

It was that last demurral that was the real grabber. The lack of electricity in the 1930's kept quite a few people away. But the old man feared it, and never permitted the house to be wired for electricity while he lived.

One of the stories that circulates around Georgetown is that Clemons used to make the renters change apartments every year so that he could equalize the strain on the foundations. Apparently he was afraid that such a condition might affect his own physical health.

On March 17, 1938, Alfred Clemons proved the fallacy of his belief in eternal life by dying. True believers like to say that the existence of a crypt, and the fact that Clemons had drawn up a will, were strong indications that he simply didn't have enough faith.

In addition to his hoard of religious paraphernalia, the old man had been a prodigious collector of all kinds of things. For instance, one of the doors of Halcyon House was supposed to have come from the old Francis Scott Key home that had stood nearby. Among the items listed in the inventory of the house when Clemons died were:

11 sandstone griffins
Samurai armor
pictures of nude women
a row of seats from Ford's Theatre
a carriage once used by President Abraham
  Lincoln

Clemons's eccentricity was also underscored in his last will and testament:

I Albert Adsit Clemons, being of sound and disposing mind and memory and not acting under duress or fraud or acting under undue influence of any person whatever, do make, publish, and declare this my last will and testament. First, I direct that upon my death having been definitely determined, the attending physician shall thereafter pierce or puncture my heart sufficiently for the purpose of absolute certainty of death.

A few occultists have pointed to Clemons's crypt and said that if he did sleep in it, then the first directive of his will must have been an attempt to clue the doctor to give a vampire eternal rest by plunging a silver instrument through his heart. They suspect that Clemons had fallen victim to a vampire that is said to have once stalked through Washington a decade before. They theorize that his obsession with religious trappings was an attempt to cure himself of the dreaded curse. Although I found accounts of the vampire's visits, I found nothing to connect Clemons to it.

Clemons's death certificate made no mention of his heart having been punctured, so it is doubtful that his wish—his last wish—was honored.

Clemons's death had a positive effect on those who rented the apartments in Halcyon House. For one thing, they were no longer required to shift apartments. The new owners wasted no time in converting the house to electricity, either. Another major undertaking was the removal of as much of the grotesque construction work as possible. Ever since Clemons's passing, there has been an effort on behalf of subsequent owners to restore as much of Halcyon House to its former state as possible. But Stoddert's house is old, and its turbulent history and the multitude of renters have left marks that can't be erased.

Most former residents have been reluctant to talk of their experiences, but enough have expressed their fears or amazement over the years to provide a fairly detailed chronicle of the goings-on in the house. Servants have been quoted, owners have been quoted, and renters have been quoted. Some have told of a figure on the stairway that vanishes whenever someone gets too close, of weird sounds echoing in the night, of unearthly shapes in rooms shrouded in darkness. There have also been reports of "an unintelligible whisper" sometimes heard floating through the once beautiful garden "on certain starry nights." It is said to come from the area where a sunken tub or pool with a large French mirror had once been located.

A few years after Clemons's death in 1938, a woman who rented one of the apartments in Halcyon House related an uncanny experience. She told of returning home from downtown to find a large engraving that hung over the mantel lying on the floor. The spike from which it had hung remained in the wall. The house had been locked up tight during

her absence and she was certain no one could have entered. Several months later, the woman returned home after a brief absence to find the engraving on the floor a second time. This time there was a big, bold black X scrawled across the face of it. The incident so frightened the woman that she fled Halcyon House and moved elsewhere.

I found a newspaper account from the 1960's about Halcyon House in which another former resident told a reporter how he was awakened by footsteps and found himself floating above his bed. The window that he had closed before retiring was wide open. The curtains fluttered in the breeze. As he debated whether to scream, try to move, or faint, he was gently lowered back onto the bed by unseen hands.

A few years later there was a similar levitation incident, this one related to me by the couple who now inhabit the part

It is from the garden of Halcyon House that whispers have been heard floating on the breeze. The beautifully terraced garden was designed by Pierre L'Enfant, and from it one could watch the ships on the Potomac River below.

of Halcyon House that Stoddert built. This couple has had many strange experiences that they don't know what to make of. Although they graciously accepted me into their home, they requested that I not use their names. They are of retirement age and they plan, after celebrating their fortieth anniversary, to move into an apartment that demands much less upkeep. Respecting their right to privacy, as journalists before me have done with previous owners, I agreed.

The husband was formerly in the foreign service, and both of these people impress me as being sober and responsible witnesses to the uncanny events they recount. They are cautious in their choice of words as they relate them, as if they don't expect others to believe what they have seen and heard. However, neither one expresses fear, nor seems tense or nervous in discussing their experiences. Halcyon House has been home to them and their children for thirteen years, and after so long a time they seem to have accepted some things that are beyond our present ability to understand.

I have talked to them, individually and together, about the house a few times over several years. "Something's a little off center," the husband will say. The wife goes further: "Someone's here. I often see him sitting here in the captain's chair." A small-framed woman with a crocheted shawl covering her shoulders, she points to the south drawing room where quite a few of the incidents have occurred. She describes the man she has seen as "balding, fat, short, an older person wearing a tan suit." His features aren't discernible and he has never spoken. She has seen him sitting there as she comes down the stairs, and once on a fall evening in 1974 he appeared while she was saying her prayers in that room. She has never seen him out of the captain's chair where he sits, "most of the time with his legs crossed." A cameo portrait of a man with a receding hairline and a round face resembling her description of the apparition hangs in the entrance hall of Halcyon House. It is a portrait of Benjamin Stoddert.

On one occasion the lady of the house has seen another man. "It was a shadowy figure dressed in black and moving very slowly," she recalls, but could provide no additional insight.

The spirit of a woman has also been reported from time to time. A few years ago the married daughter and daughter-in-law of the owners told them of seeing the face of an old woman in an upstairs window. They had spotted it from the patio in the garden that was designed by Pierre L'Enfant. Then during a visit a few months later, one of the grandchildren, a six-year-old, began to cry out in the evenings long after he was supposed to be asleep. When someone would come to his bedroom to comfort him, he would

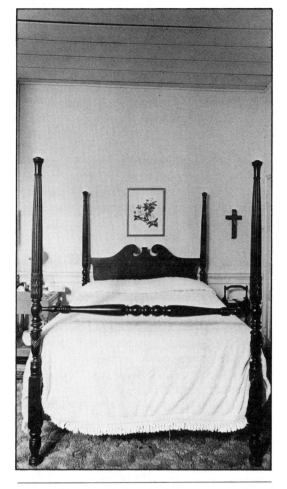

From this second-floor bedroom come tales of levitation and of footsteps that can be heard in the attic above.

say that he had been frightened by an old woman who kept waking him up by rearranging his bedcovers. One morning at breakfast the child beamed and said, "Guess what?" Then he told everyone he didn't have to worry about being scared by the old woman anymore. He said she had visited him the night before and whispered, "Don't worry, I won't return." With that she kissed him, and, according to his story, disappeared out of the second-story window.

No one in Halcyon House has seen her since.

The children of the couple who live in the house seem to have received some of their parents' calmness when it comes to dealing with the ghosts of Halcyon

22 House. At first, naturally, the goings-on
were quite novel—even scary. Within a
few years, one of the sons wrote about
what it was like living in a haunted
house for *Parade Magazine*.

One incident that he related involved
a light that he had seen burning in the
basement. When he called out, "Who's
there?" the light went out. Filled with
what he described as "a blood-chilling
dread," he yelled for his father to get the
police. The police could find no one
there. The light switch worked perfectly
and the young man said no one could
have gotten out because he was guarding
the only exit.

Many of the other occurrences he described in that April 21, 1963, article still
go on as they have for more than a
hundred years. "Lights go out, but we
just turn them on again," the lady of the
house says matter-of-factly.

The master bedroom is still the scene
of many inexplicable happenings, such as
the levitation that was reported in the
newspaper account. This time a young
lady, who was a guest, was assigned the
room. She was awakened in the middle
of the night by a feeling of weightless-
ness, and realized she was actually suspended in midair above the bed. Too
frightened to move or scream, she felt invisible, clammy hands slowly turn and
lower her. When she rested on the bed
again, her feet were on the pillow.

The woman of the house smiles as she
thinks about another incident that happened in 1972 when relatives who were
house-sitting for the weekend were given
the master bedroom to sleep in. The first
day was uneventful, but the next morning, the man and his wife awoke to dis-
cover they had been reversed while sleeping, and their heads were resting at the
foot of the bed.

Then the couple told me about a
young college student who slept in the
room three years later when he was also
house-sitting. The couple had recommended that he sleep in the master bedroom because it was air-conditioned and
had a phone. That evening, the young
man had a few friends in. When they
left, he showered and went to sleep. At
2 A.M. he phoned his family in McLean,
Virginia, and told them he was coming

Benjamin Stoddert's ghost has often been seen sitting in the captain's chair on the right.

24 home. The next day, he phoned the couple and volunteered to check the house three times a day, but vowed he would not come back at night. He never told them what had frightened him so much.

Above the room, which some think was Benjamin Stoddert's bedroom, is one of the attics from which have emanated the ghostly noises reported by scores of people over the years. The present owner has heard noises, he told me as he showed me the master bedroom. It sounds like "a person walking or running up there." He was looking up at the lowered ceiling. "But I'm not going to get up and see. I don't care." I thought of other accounts I have heard and read about the strange noises and tappings from the attic, and about lights going out, but the man of the house views these and the other nocturnal occurrences as eccentricities of an aging

and decaying house. "We've enjoyed living here and our extrasensory companions, if any, certainly haven't upset me any," he says.

Oblivious to the tales of revisits from departed residents, the federal government once considered taking on the restoration of Halcyon House. In the mid-1960's they sent architects and housing experts to examine the old home, because it was being considered as a home for Vice President Hubert Humphrey. The plans were abandoned, however, on the advice of the experts. The architectural authorities said that the atrocities of Clemons, the weather, and the years had taken too great a toll to make restoration feasible. They pointed to giant cracks that had opened in the wall overlooking the garden, to thick supporting timbers that had been placed inside the drawing room and the dining room to prevent the

ceiling from crashing down. But no one will ever really know if that was the only reason, or whether they were frightened off by the report of things that go bump in the night, as many others have been.

Whatever the infirmities of Halcyon House, it still has a special aura about it. The moment you enter the house you sense the inner conflict. Looking closely you may see evidence of the beautiful home Benjamin Stoddert planned, but the garish decoration wrought by Clemons—which, unfortunately, cannot be hidden—predominates. You also see the attempts at restoration made by owners who followed Clemons.

Some believe that the spirits of Clemons and Stoddert prowl their old home. The ghost of Stoddert is dressed in tan, that of Clemons in black. Should they be correct, I shudder at the thought that one day the spirit of Stoddert may en-

counter the spirit of the eccentric who maimed his beloved Halcyon House. That turbulence just may be too much for the old building to withstand.

THE SINISTER SPECTER OF FRANCIS SCOTT KEY

The northeast exit ramp of the Key Bridge was built on the spot where the home of the man who wrote "The Star-Spangled Banner" used to stand. Some say the planners named the bridge after

This photo, taken just after the turn of the century, gives little hint of what was going on inside of Francis Scott Key's former house on M Street.

26 Francis Scott Key in order to quell his angry spirit.

Key had been a practicing attorney in Georgetown when he lived in the home, and he maintained his law office there. From the rear of the house, which had been built in 1802, he could see the majestic Potomac. No doubt his mind would sometimes go back to the brief period when he had been a prisoner on board a British ship in Baltimore Harbor during the bombardment of Fort McHenry. The violence of battles that had inspired him then must have seemed an eternity away as he looked out over the peaceful Potomac.

It is unfortunate that those who took over the Key house after the noted attorney lived there did not share his concern for the property. During the thirty years Key lived there, the house had been well maintained; about the only concern later owners had was to maintain Key's name. After all, such famous property had no trouble attracting renters—keeping them was the problem.

You see, the house was filled with what various newspaper articles described as "sinister sounds." I found a couple of accounts—one in a newspaper of the late 1800's and another just after the turn of the century—that described the house as haunted. Both reports said that the noises began a short time after Key died. Floors creaked when no one could be seen walking on them. Doors squeaked. Rafters seemed to moan.

In the early 1920's one family lived there who "refused to be driven from the home in spite of the occurrences." According to a newspaper account, the house had previously been vacant for "prolonged periods." After several sleepless nights, the new occupants launched a widespread search throughout the old house in an effort to learn where the noises that were keeping them awake were coming from. The reporter said they discovered a section of the attic not previously known about, and on the ceiling there found dried bloodstains, but little else. That night moans unlike any they had ever heard reverberated from the attic—forcing them to change their minds and decide that moving was not such a bad idea after all. Just how the stains got

Some say it was the spirit of Francis Scott Key that haunted his Georgetown house in the hopes of scaring the owners into restoring the property to its former condition.

on the attic ceiling remains a mystery.

Renters came and renters went, but the decay of the Key house continued. Some actually say the sounds and omens increased as the deterioration of the house spread. A few people wanted to tear it down and rid Georgetown of an eyesore—a haunted eyesore at that. However, the owners were finally persuaded to make a serious attempt to restore the house to its previous state—the condition it had been in when Key lived there. Their efforts met with tremendous success in more ways than one—the sinister sounds ceased when restoration was completed.

Is it possible that the erratic noises came from the restless spirit of Key, upset over the lack of concern and care for the home he had so loved? Perhaps, but I have never been able to get those old bloodstains out of my mind. One old-timer told me that even when the restoration was completed—and that included the painting of the attic ceiling—the old bloodstains continued to show through the paint. What harrowing act caused them? When? Had Key been involved?

The house that spawned those questions is no more. It was torn down in the name of progress to make way for access ramps for the Whitehurst Freeway and a span across the Potomac. There was quite a bit of debate at the time about whether the old Key house should be demolished. Nevertheless, the advocates of concrete and steel won out. Virginia commuters got their bridge (named after Francis Scott Key, of course), and Georgetown and the nation lost a historic, albeit haunted, landmark.

TEN O'CLOCK RITUAL AT FOXALL

Foxall stands in stately splendor just about a block off Georgetown's busy shopping street, Wisconsin Avenue, on Dumbarton Avenue, where the limbs of massive trees both obscure and protect the several homes that have risen up around this sturdily constructed relic. There was a time when Foxall was revisited by a spirit who performed what old-timers refer to as "the ten o'clock ritual."

This handsome mansion was the pride of Thomas Jefferson's dear friend Henry Foxall, who had come to Washington from Philadelphia at the insistence of Jefferson. The two men, both violinists, often enjoyed relaxing there in the evenings with their music. The Virginian had talked Foxall into building the Columbian Ordnance Foundry on the river just below what is now Georgetown University, and Foxall prospered. His foundry supplied many of the cannons for the American forces in the War of 1812.

A few years after the war—when his only surviving child married Samuel McKinney—Foxall gave her the Dumbarton Avenue home. It really isn't known when the so-called "ten o'clock ritual" began. I read newspaper accounts from late in the last century that told of a room in "a house in Georgetown that was cursed with darkness every evening at ten." Various other articles in newspapers and books have also mentioned the phenomenon, which defied candles, gaslight, and for a number of years, electricity too.

Several references to encounters with "a diaphanous, aged woman" have been reported. Most who had encountered her said that she floated through the third-floor hallway, but vanished if they approached. All of her recorded appearances were "just before ten P.M." Her description has stimulated speculation among some old Georgetowners, who say that she resembles a daguerreotype of a housekeeper who had served Foxall families for a number of years. The most often repeated legend is that all the families she had served during her life at Foxall had used the third floor as the children's floor. They say that as housekeeper she enforced the rule of "lights out at ten" and that even after death, sometime before the turn of the century, she returned to perform her "nightly ritual."

No one with whom I talked seemed to know just when the last incident had been reported. Newspaper references to the legend since the early 1950's seem to be retelling previous accounts of the 1920's and 1930's, and even go back to when the first stories appeared in the last century. Only the long-time neighbors could even recall the legend, and none with whom I talked admitted ever having witnessed the ten o'clock blackout. I also spoke with Foxall's current owner, who has lived there with his family since 1955. He said that his children, when hearing of the legend, had tried on "several occasions" to get the little old lady back. "They even reverted to candle power, but nothing. Absolutely nothing." He added with a smile, "We've never had any indication the place was haunted."

THE GHOST OF THE MURDERED MADAM

There is one old house, perhaps gone now, that was constructed somewhere on 35th Street in Northwest Washington just after the Revolution, where swishing sounds, described as similar to those made by the starched petticoats worn by the women of the early or mid-1800's, were said to precede whoever climbed the stairs during certain evening hours. Old newspaper accounts quote visitors who said that after following the sounds upstairs, they had glimpsed a "shadowy substance slipping into a room at the top of the stairs." There is no record of any shade ever preceding anyone *down* those stairs.

I was told, but not surprisingly was not able to confirm, that the old house was once one of Georgetown's finer brothels. The madam prided herself on maintaining a small, but select, group of girls who were not only lovely to look at, but excellent conversationalists—should a customer desire that as well. Legend relates that the madam came to Georgetown as a runaway from an old Atlanta plantation. She had been the daughter of a rich, but dictatorial, southern planter who had caught her with a handsome field hand in the hayloft of the barn. Before the young man could reach for his pants, the father shot him dead. He severely beat the girl, and then carried her back to the mansion, where he locked her inside her room. In the darkness of night, the southern belle put a few things together and climbed out her window. She was never seen again in that area.

The story of what had happened spread throughout the county. Field hand told field hand, house servants told their masters. The girl had brought disgrace to her father; but worse, in the mind of the young man to whom she was betrothed, she had dishonored *him*. The young man was ridiculed everywhere. His friends wouldn't let him forget that his girl had taken up with a slave. He awoke one morning to find a bale of hay at his front door. He blamed his former fiancée for destroying his life. As his hatred for the girl he once loved grew, he resolved to get revenge, and set off to find her.

The young woman had tried to hide her trail. She went to Macon—far south of Atlanta—before boarding a stage north. Also traveling by the same stage, according to the legend, was a member of Georgia's delegation to Congress. The two became very close on that grueling stage ride, and the congressman found the girl not only attractive but intelligent.

She confessed to her middle-aged companion that she was running away from home but concealed the hayloft adventure. The congressman was more than sympathetic. When they arrived in the Nation's Capital, he suggested an inexpensive yet respectable ladies' boarding house for the young girl. He promised to call on her again soon and, if possible, to help her obtain some form of employment.

The young woman had ideas of her own on how to make it in the big city. She became more than a friend to her stagecoach companion, and before too many weeks passed had talked the gentleman out of a large sum of money in order to purchase her own home in Georgetown. As the months went by, she kept her ears and eyes opened. Her great charm made her an instant success at several of the functions the Georgia congressman escorted her to.

One evening, after a most satisfying dinner and a carriage ride down by Rock Creek, the young woman unveiled her plan to her ally. She would open a discreet brothel, employing only cultured women capable of satisfying a man's mind as well as his body. She personally vowed to be faithful only to her congressman.

At first the Georgia politician was reluctant, but his mistress had a way of making him change his mind. They spent several months organizing and quietly letting it be known that a new and most unusual place was about to open. From the beginning the lavishly decorated brothel was a success. Months passed but the initial success did not fade. Perhaps it was because neither the congressman nor his consort was greedy. They were content to keep the brothel small, employing only four girls and concentrating on quality. Quality in companionship. Quality in clientele.

It was late one spring evening four years later when a routine knock on the door was answered by the madam. She screamed. Standing in the doorway cursing and spitting out vile language at the top of his voice was the man her father had chosen for her to marry long ago in Atlanta.

His face was weather-beaten and unshaven, his broad shoulders rounded from the hours he had spent outdoors in the saddle. He grabbed her wrist. The hatred that had been pent up inside him for five years seemed to explode as he slapped her across the face. The force of the slap broke his hold on her arm. The woman spun loose and raced back into the house. He chased her.

Two employees and a man in the parlor were startled by the commotion. They stood speechless, watching as the crazed intruder chased the screaming woman up the stairs shouting profanities about her last days on her father's plantation.

He cornered her in the room just off the top of the stairs. Another scream erupted, but died as though choked off. That's when the others were jarred into action and rushed up the stairs. They were too late.

Lying on the floor was the crumpled body of the madam. Her throat still bore finger marks. Tears still glistened on her cheeks. The window on the far side of the room was open. The curtains fluttered in the night breeze. There was no one else in the room. Legend has it that the murderer got away. The congressman moved behind the scenes to sell the house, hoping that it would help him to forget his lost love, and what had happened to her there.

Down through the years, though, it seemed that the spirit of the disgraced young woman couldn't forget that last climb up the stairs, and so climbed them again and again, disappearing into the room at the top, hoping each time that the outcome would be different.

THE HAUNTED HOUSES OF TWO DIPLOMATS

I discovered four or five other Georgetown ghosts of the past, but the original newspaper accounts are vague, and I have been unable to uncover additional details. Two involve members of the diplomatic corps from foreign nations. Quite a few diplomats stationed in Washington have found Georgetown an attractive place to live. They have also found that the shield of diplomatic immunity doesn't protect them from visits from local spirits. As yet there have been no international incidents caused by any of these visitations, but some have done nothing to foster better foreign relations.

A diplomat, identified in accounts only as a "former Portuguese minister," once occupied an old home that was haunted by the spirit of a "long dead British soldier." A newspaper article from the 1930's didn't say where in Georgetown the old house was located, or how long ago "once" was. The writer doesn't even tell us whether the apparition was a soldier from the Revolutionary War or from the War of 1812.

The account relates how the minister's wife encountered the ghost early one morning in the hallway. She told the reporter that she first thought it was a servant who had also risen early, but when it drew closer, her blood ran cold as she realized that the thing coming at her was not of this world. The soldier, whom she described as having a rather pale and haggard look, continued to approach. The frightened woman became fixed to the spot. The scream she tried to muster caught in her throat. She flattened her body against the wall. She told the reporter she began to feel faint. As unconsciousness was overtaking her, the wistful eyes of that ghostly pale face stared into hers. She remembered that as she crumpled to the floor, she felt the cold, clammy touch of the soldier's hand as he apparently reached out for her elbow in an attempt to prevent her from falling. It took her several days under a doctor's care to recover from the experience. The diplomat and his wife moved shortly thereafter, and to my knowledge no other

article was ever written about that house
and its ghost.

A Russian diplomat complained of
tapping sounds at the ground level windows of his old Georgetown home, according to a 1920's newspaper article.
The story told of the minister's annoy-
ance at being interrupted during late evening hours as he tried to work on affairs
of state, and of his being kept awake
some nights. Having survived several
purges by the Czar just before the Russian Revolution, the minister wasn't easily frightened. As a matter of fact, I got
the idea from the article that he suspected the noises might have been an attempt at communication from the after-
world, and he was interested in studying
the phenomenon.

The article said that he often took lantern in hand and personally investigated
the annoyances. The Russian minister
was forced to conclude that it was something other than the neighborhood children having fun when he came upon
some startling evidence one rainy night.
Almost with the first tapping sound, the
minister grabbed his lantern and bolted
from the house to the window where the
sound had come from. He found no foot-
prints, yet wherever he stepped he left a
deep print in the soft ground of the
flower bed beneath the window. Knowing
the history of the house, the diplomat
theorized that the tapping sounds could
have been made by the spirit of some
long-dead slave who had been killed
while tapping on the window of a house
he had wrongly suspected of being part
of the Underground Railroad.

SPIRITS OF
GEORGETOWN BRIDGES

Georgetown is bordered on the east by
Rock Creek and on the south by the Potomac. The bridges over these two water-
ways have spawned some interesting
stories over the years.

One of the bridges that spanned Rock
Creek was a long wooden affair. It no
longer stands, but for years Georgetowners shuddered at some of the tales spun
around two accidents. One of the stories
went back to the era just after the Revolution. It involved a drummer boy. The
youth was from "nearby Falls Church,"
according to most accounts. One windy
day as he crossed the bridge, a great gust
of wind blew him off balance, and he
tumbled over the side and drowned. His
body was never found. There were reports of muffled drumbeats being carried
on the air currents for several years
thereafter. An article in one Georgetown
publication, which retells the story, said,
"There are residents who insist that when
the nights are quiet and Rock Creek is
but a babble, one may hear the muffled
roll of a drum trembling in the air." The
sound supposedly begins faintly, from far
away, but grows ever louder as it reaches
the area of the bridge where the youth
fell over the side. Then—there is silence.

The other incident involving that same
Rock Creek bridge occurred many years
later. The wooden span had become
rather rickety with age but was still used.
One night, during a fierce storm, the old
relic collapsed just as a stagecoach went
thundering across. The driver and the
horses met their death in the swollen,
muddy waters below.

For years after that incident, whispers
drifted around the Georgetown wharf,
through the pubs, and among people on
the streets that the drama continued to
be re-enacted on certain starless nights.
Fear could be detected in the voices of
those living near where the old bridge
used to be as they would recall in somber tones what they had glimpsed on
more than one stormy night.

They told of a ghostly coach, with a
driver who whipped his horses in panic
as he tried to cross a bridge that was no
longer there. The "aphonic" apparition
always vanished in a clap of thunder and
a flash of lightning in what would have
been the middle of the bridge.

These stories began to die out within a
few decades after the collapse of the
rickety old span. Apparently, without the
bridge as a reminder, Georgetowners
didn't think about the incidents so often.
Besides, another nearby bridge was vying
for attention, and its ghost was much
more frightening.

The old K Street Bridge was one of

The Long Bridge

the spans most frequently used by travel-
ers from Georgetown. It too had a legend that persisted over the years it stood,
although the number of reports dimin-
ished after electricity brightened the
nearby streets, and stores and shops replaced its wooded approaches. Nevertheless, there were those who feared street
crime much less than an encounter with
the horrible "headless man of the K
Street Bridge."

The stories of this macabre apparition
first sprang up in the last century. Seldom did anyone who encountered the
disembodied spirit ever return to travel
the bridge again. At its very mention, fear
would be reflected in their eyes.

It has been difficult to determine just
how this phantom came to haunt the
bridge, or for that matter, how he lost
his head. I have heard a couple of theo-
ries. One that was put forth in an old
newspaper account surmised that the

*Long Bridge where a Union patrol is supposed
to have encountered Braddock's spectral
army on its never-ending march.*

phantom had lost his head "in noble battle during the War between the States."
Seldom was he ever referred to elsewhere
in such sympathetic tones. It was obvious
that the writer had never come in contact
with the specter, nor had he ever met anyone else who had.

More often the accounts expressed a
belief that the silent spirit of the K Street
Bridge was the victim of punishment for
some heinous crime. Some even conjectured that the beheading had been carried out by vigilantes. Actually, those citizens who had the misfortune to meet the
headless ghost of the K Street Bridge
seldom took time to wonder how he had
lost his head. They were only anxious
that he not take theirs before they could
escape.

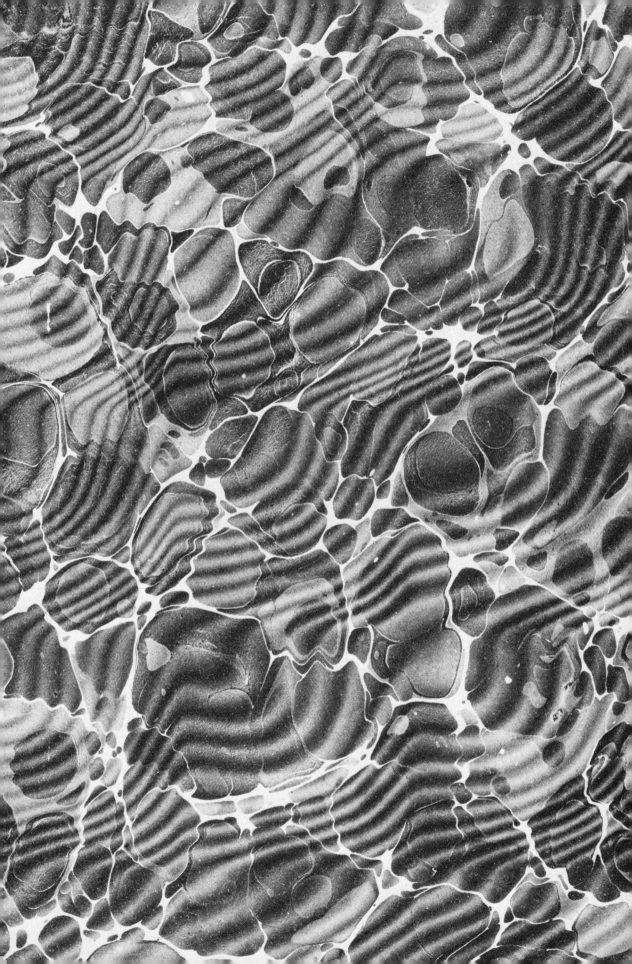

2. LAFAYETTE SQUARE

The most heavily traveled route from Georgetown into the District is now a couple of blocks north of K Street. Traveling east on M Street and then on Pennsylvania Avenue to Washington Circle, and continuing on Pennsylvania Avenue for seven blocks, will take you to Lafayette Square.

The square across from the White House has not always carried the name of the Frenchman who fought bravely for American independence. For many years after construction of the President's House (as the White House was first known), the square across the street was known as "The President's Square." As you read these tales involving many of the residents of the square, you may find yourself in agreement with Washingtonians who refer to it as "Tragedy Square."

No other section of Washington has had so much intrigue, mystery, murder, and macabre happenings as has the area directly opposite 1600 Pennsylvania Avenue. Few of the original homes of the square remain, and that may partially explain the turbulence of the spirits who revisit their old neighborhood.

THE SIX GREAT WASHINGTONIANS OF ST. JOHN'S CHURCH

The first structure erected on Lafayette Square (aside from the White House) was St. John's Church. It was designed by Benjamin Latrobe, who topped the steeple with a one-thousand-pound bell. Completed in 1821, the church has counted many American Presidents among those who have attended services there.

The sanctuary is almost always open, and those who enter sense that they are not only in a house of worship, but in a house shrouded in history. The pews, of a deep, rich hardwood, are the same ones parishioners have sat on for more than 150 years.

Legend has it that when the large old bell tolls the death of a famous man, the white-robed spirits of "six great Washingtonians," whose names have been obscured by time, appear at midnight. They sit in the pew of the Presidents with arms folded and heads facing forward, pay

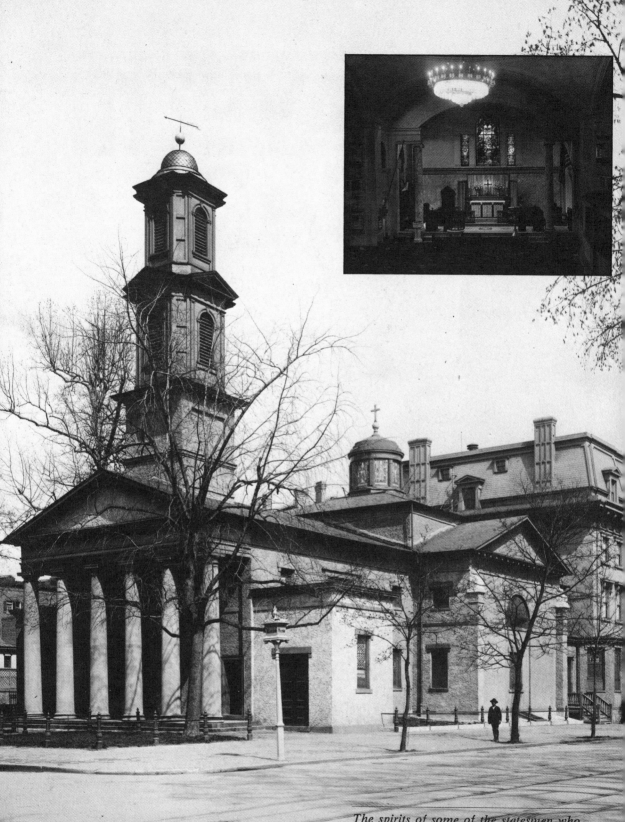

The spirits of some of the statesmen who worshipped at St. John's Church materialize whenever one of America's leaders dies. The ghosts of great Americans make their way to the Pew of the Presidents, pay their respects, and vanish.

their respects, and vanish as silently as they appeared.

When the hour is late and the moon bright enough, some say you can see Dolley Madison rocking on the porch of this house on Lafayette Square, where she spent her last days.

DOLLEY MADISON'S PERIPATETIC SPIRIT

There was a time when anyone who was anyone, or had ambitions to achieve greatness, lived or was entertained in one or more of the houses on the President's Square. Cabinet members, congressional leaders, representatives of the diplomatic corps, newspaper publishers, admirals, generals, presidential aspirants, men of the judiciary, beautiful women of society, and men-about-town gathered here.

Among the early residents of the square was the noted philanthropist and art collector William Corcoran. Another was Dolley Madison, who spent her declining years in the house that still stands

on the corner of what is now Madison and H Streets, Northwest. She revisits the old house even now. Late at night men leaving the popular Washington Club when it was a few doors down the street used to report tipping their hats to the spirit of Mrs. Madison, which could be seen rocking in the shadows of her porch. Dolley's spirit is one of the most active in Washington. It has also been seen in the White House gardens and at the Octagon, but then Dolley's life was quite active, too.

The Dolley Madison house is by no means the only one on Lafayette Square where encounters with the spirit world have been reported.

STEPHEN DECATUR'S DISASTROUS DUEL

Stephen Decatur, America's favorite hero of the early 1800's, was in his mid thirties and had the two Barbary Wars behind him when he and his wife, Susan, moved to Washington. At the time that the handsome, rich, and idolized naval hero decided to build a home on Lafayette Square, only the President's House and St. John's Church were there.

Decatur so loved his new home, designed by the much-sought-after architect Benjamin Latrobe, and had so many happy moments there with his wife, that it is said he frequently returns to the elegant brick home—still standing at Jefferson Place and now the headquarters for the National Trust for Historic Preservation. Perhaps he is searching for an answer to how he could have lost his life when he had so much to live for.

Decatur was from a family of seafarers out of Sinepuxent, Maryland. He served in the Caribbean as a lieutenant during the undeclared naval hostilities with France when the new Navy under Secretary Benjamin Stoddert was flexing its muscles. He also proved himself in the Mediterranean, and in 1803 was given command of his first ship. By the next year the swashbuckling Marylander had destroyed the captured American frigate *Philadelphia* in Tripoli Harbor. That

Stephen Decatur, whose brilliant career was cut short by a duel.

earned him a captaincy, and kept tales of his exploits circulating through the remainder of the war. Word of his brilliance and courage in combat reached port ahead of his returning ship. Hampton Roads was buzzing about Stephen Decatur. He was lionized by Norfolk society, and it was there that he met Susan Wheeler, daughter of the mayor. Five months later they were married.

A year or so after their marriage, an incident occurred on the high seas—not directly involving Decatur—that eventually led to his premature death.

It had been a quarter of a century since the United States had fought Britain for independence, yet British ships sometimes still tried unsuccessfully to intimidate American vessels on the high seas. The balance changed, however,

Stephen Decatur's house, designed by Benjamin Latrobe, still stands on Lafayette Square. Although the first-floor window on H Street appears to just be shuttered, it is actually walled up—supposedly in an unsuccessful attempt to prevent the Commodore's apparition from returning to stare out the window in the bedroom where he died.

when the British frigate *Leopard* encountered the American frigate *Chesapeake*. The *Leopard*'s commander fired one shot across the bow of the *Chesapeake,* and that was all it took for the *Chesapeake*'s Commodore, James Barron, to allow a boarding party to remove four sailors that the British charged were deserters from His Majesty's Royal Navy. Word of the incident spread rapidly.

When Barron sailed his frigate back into Norfolk, he was greeted with an order for a court-martial. The nine-member board, which included Stephen Decatur, suspended Barron from the Navy for five years on charges that he had failed to clear his ship for action. The *Chesapeake-Leopard* incident proved to be the slow-burning fuse that ignited the War of 1812 five years later.

Commodore Barron never quite forgave Decatur for his role in that court-martial. No doubt the fact that the Navy named Decatur commander of the *Chesapeake* explains, at least in part, why Barron singled him out from the others on that board as a target for his resentment. Decatur sailed off toward more heroic exploits in the War of 1812, and the embittered Barron, exiled from the Navy, plotted his adversary's death.

At the war's end, the laurels of Washington awaited the courageous naval strategist, and there is no doubt that Decatur could have realized any political ambitions he might have had. He and his wife, Susan, moved to the capital. Decatur's exploits on the high seas kept the conversation going at many social gatherings. There were few men in Washington, or elsewhere, who could rival the Commodore. His charm and poise, added to his reputation for heroism, were more than enough to captivate the ladies of the Federal City's society. Husbands were just as enamored of the beautiful and soft-spoken Susan as their wives were of Decatur.

Susan Decatur was overjoyed to have her husband home, but being at home was a new and different life-style for the seagoing Commodore, and for his part, it took some getting used to. Marie T. Beall writes in her book *Decatur House and Its Inhabitants* that it was difficult for the Commodore to cope with such peaceful surroundings. The restless Decatur once complained in a letter to a friend that there were no signs of war, and revealed how ashamed he would be "to die in my bed."

Had Commodore James Barron known of Decatur's boredom he might have moved more quickly. Barron's hostility toward Decatur had increased each time he was thwarted in his attempt at getting the command of another ship. He had been reinstated in the Navy at half pay after his suspension expired, but he was always passed over for the posts he sought. Barron was convinced that Decatur was the source of the opposition he was meeting with, and he mounted a campaign to provoke Decatur into a duel.

It wasn't easy. Although Decatur had fought several duels earlier in his life, there are indications that he was not eager to return to the field of honor. But the vengeful Barron was persistent, and Decatur could ignore his personal attacks no longer. Reluctantly, Decatur wrote to his nemesis: ". . . if we fight, it must be on your own seeking." The letter was touted by Barron as Decatur's acceptance to do battle.

Legend has it that on the eve of the duel that was finally arranged between Decatur and Barron, there was a party at the Decatur house, but Decatur didn't seem to be in the mood to join in the festivities. Oppressed by a feeling of approaching doom, he walked into his bedroom and over to a window facing the north, where he sadly gazed out over his estate. His marriage was entering its fifteenth year, but the past fourteen months had held special significance. He and Susan had spent them peacefully in their new home. The smell of gunpowder had never seemed so remote.

Killing Barron would not improve Decatur's reputation, nor did he believe that Barron could profit by his death. Stephen Decatur had survived a naval career spanning four wars. He had fought hand to hand while boarding vessels on the high seas. He had seen his brother fall dead at his side. His best friend had chosen to be blown to bits in a shipboard explosion rather than be captured. Decatur had faced death many times before. He faced it now again.

Before the sun could break through the darkness on the morning of March 14, 1820, Decatur slipped from his wife's warm side to meet his destiny. His friend William Bainbridge met him in the square. They rode in somber silence out the Baltimore Road across the District of Columbia boundary line, and stopped in a field near the small Maryland town of Bladensburg. The predawn sound of the crickets was drowned out by the birds that had begun to sing. A few yards away a brook called Blood Run trickled by the edge of the notorious dueling field.

The morning serenity was pierced by the occasional clicking of metal on metal as the two men checked their weapons. The duel was at eight paces—murderously close. Presumably, this was a concession to the nearsighted Barron.

As first light tinted the sky, Bainbridge recited the instructions: The men could not fire before the count of one, nor after the count of three. Witnesses reported that two shots sounded as one when Bainbridge reached the count of two.

Barron fell immediately with a bullet in his hip. Many argue that Decatur was not off target and that he never intended to kill Barron.

Decatur stood there, pistol smoking, staring down at the fallen Barron, who lay in agony almost at his feet. Decatur was not smiling. The naval hero winced in pain, put his hand to his right side, and fell.

The mortally wounded Decatur was brought back to his home on the President's Square. One account of the tragedy said that his wife Susan was so paralyzed by his condition that she could not bring herself to see him. Decatur knew he was dying, and his last words were, "If it were in the cause of my country, it would be nothing."

The nation lost one of its greatest heroes that night. Flags flew at half-mast, and Decatur's funeral cortege passed through the streets of Washington, where thousands stood in mourning. Despite the manner of his death, he was buried with full military honors. Later, towns in Georgia, Illinois, and Alabama would be named for him.

A year after the Commodore's death,

Susan Wheeler Decatur could not bring herself to look at her mortally wounded husband when he was brought home, and after his death she could not bear to stay in the house they had shared. One writer said, "Mrs. Decatur's grief was viewed as somewhat exaggerated even in her own day." Legend has it that at times she can still be heard weeping for her lost husband.

some of the household staff were returning home late one night and saw Decatur's spirit as it made its first appearance at that same window where he had stood on the evening before his death.

The window was ordered walled up. But that did not prevent what one journalist of the past century called "the adumbral Decatur" from revisiting his home to look over what had been his elegant estate. His transparent form has been reported on numerous occasions since. Passers-by on H Street who have claimed to have spotted it at the walled-up window describe his expression as melancholy. Some household staff members earlier in the century attested to having seen a transparent figure silently slipping out the back door just before dawn, with a black box under its arm—just as Stephen Decatur did that March morning in 1820 when he left to meet Commodore James Barron on the field of honor at Bladensburg.

40

THE ATTORNEY GENERAL'S MIDNIGHT CALLERS

Somewhere just to the north and west of Lafayette Square there once stood another of the Federal District houses that attracted those in the higher echelons of government. As a matter of fact, a former Attorney General and the Supreme Court Chief Justice before whom he had argued a great many historic cases were said to be among those who continued to frequent the home for many years after their death.

Tales were being whispered about the house even before Aaron V. Brown moved in, in the 1850's. The former Tennessee governor had served three terms in Congress and was no stranger to Washington. Now, Brown was to be Postmaster General under President James Buchanan. He and his wife, Cynthia, felt proud to have found such a historic house. One article I read said that Brown used to boast to friends about its having belonged to Attorney General William Wirt, who had served Presidents James Madison and John Quincy Adams. Brown used to tell his guests about the famous people who had visited his home—South Carolina's John C.

Calhoun, Speaker of the House Henry Clay, Daniel Webster, and fellow Tennessean Andrew Jackson.

After he had lived in the house a short time, however, Brown's personality began to change. Those close to him noticed that he had become rather edgy, often grumpy, and that he complained with increasing frequency of noises keeping him awake at night. One reporter said that he bickered with his household staff about their late hours, but they pleaded innocence.

None of the servants had seen a soul stirring in the midnight hours, but several said that they had heard strange voices drifting through the halls on more than one moonless night, and that they too had trouble sleeping at night. There are indications that they began to return to their own homes to sleep. Brown wrongfully assumed that he would get more sleep with the servants gone. Dark circles began to appear under his eyes. One story dwelt on how short his temper was with his staff members. He seldom smiled anymore.

One newspaper account I read said that the Postmaster General was convinced that former owner Attorney General Wirt was returning to his home on certain nights to discuss and argue law with former Chief Justice John Marshall and other long-dead political figures. It was while Marshall was Chief Justice that one of the Supreme Court's most momentous precedents was set, allowing the court to declare an act of Congress unconstitutional. This expanded the powers of the still-new federal government while restricting those of the states. According to legend, it was this action that summoned the spirits of the country's most fervent States' rightists to the Wirt home. Among those voices raised in ethereal debate, witnesses claimed to have heard South Carolina's firebrand John C. Calhoun's oratorical tones and Virginia's "eccentric and rhetorical Congressman

*William Wirt (left) and John Marshall (right)
are just two of the ethereal visitors said to have
disturbed the sleep of Aaron Brown as they
argued about State's Rights in Wirt's old home.*

John Randolph's shrill—almost soprano
—voice."

The way Brown was running the Post
Office Department was becoming an increasingly open scandal. "The morals
that characterized his administration of
the Post Office were deplorable," says
Gerald Cullinan in his book *The Post
Office Department,* adding, "Politics was
everything." Among the outrages: a
swindling New York postmaster was permitted to "escape" to Mexico with
$155,000 in postal funds because, Cullinan says, he was a "sterling Democratic
politician." By 1858 Brown had run up
record budget deficits for the postal service. Was his work affecting his home life,
or was his home life affecting his work?

It is certain that the strange voices he
heard drifting through the blackness of
his house greatly disturbed the Postmaster General until his sudden death. The
Washington Star of March 8, 1859, says
Brown "suffered from a painful illness of
some ten days duration." The Postmaster

General died that same morning. All
public business was suspended, and he
lay in state in the East Room of the
White House. Speculation at the time
that Brown went crazy and then began
hearing voices seems unfounded. Articles
describing other encounters in the old
Wirt house continued after his death.
Apparently, until it was torn down there
was no letup in the supernatural sessions.
The disturbing noises were said to have
driven one owner to suicide, but since he
left no note, no one knows the real reason he ended his life. And no one will
ever know whether demolition of the old
home forced Wirt and Marshall to argue
elsewhere with their cronies, or whether
the adversaries of the past settled their
dispute.

THE REVENGE OF THE CUCKOLDED HUSBAND

Above from left to right: Daniel Sickles, Theresa Sickles, and Philip Barton Key. Key's restless spirit still is known to haunt Lafayette Square.

In 1859 Washington's social foundations were rocked by a shocking scandal involving the flamboyant Daniel Sickles and Philip Barton Key, the son of the composer of the national anthem. How they became two of Washington's most noticeable ghosts is a story worth retelling.

Sickles was a good-looking former congressman from New York. He had been married for a little over five years to the beautiful daughter of an Italian music teacher. Theresa Sickles was described in *Harper's Weekly* as "very pretty and girlish and extremely attractive in manner; well-educated, and charming in every way."

After his marriage, Sickles was "without office" for a few years. He latched onto a job in the Foreign Service and spent some time in London. When he and his wife returned to Washington, he immediately channeled his energies into James Buchanan's campaign for President and in winning back the seat he had once held in Congress. They moved into a home on Lafayette Square and threw themselves into the city's social whirl. Twice weekly the Sickles wined and dined the influential of Washington. Lafayette Square was the hub of the city's social and political circles, yet few houses on the square could boast as much carriage traffic as that of the Sickles.

Although Theresa Sickles was only seventeen when she married Sickles, he knew then she would be an asset to his career. A *Harper's* reporter said, "She was soul and charm of these affairs. There was something inexpressibly fascinating about her fresh girlish face, and her sweet amiable manner."

Yet, after he had won back his seat in Congress, Sickles spent considerable time in his home district with his constituents, and though he seemed to find time to appreciate the belles of the District of Columbia, he didn't have much time for his wife. At the Sickles's soirees, Daniel Sickles was often in the company of other women or listening to some politician or lobbyist. But as time went on, his wife began to spend her time with the handsome widower Philip Barton Key. Before he married, Key had been described as "a renowned lady's man," and *Harper's* said, "as a widower his ancient prestige returned to him."

From almost the first meeting the couple seemed inseparable. "At balls, at parties, in the street, at receptions, at theatres, everywhere, Mrs. Sickles invariably is accompanied by Philip Barton Key, District Attorney," said one newspaper of the day. Key seemed to add sparkle to Theresa Sickles's life. She smiled more often and her eyes twinkled

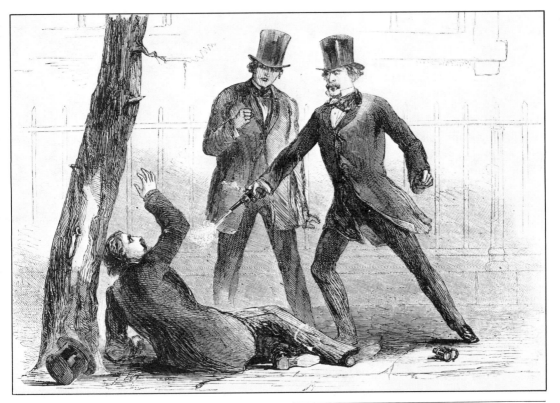

In the scene above from a drawing in Harper's Weekly *irate husband Daniel Sickles shot and killed Philip Barton Key as he was on his way to a rendezvous with Sickles's wife.*

as they had not in years.

The *Harper's* writer suggested that neither Mr. Key nor Mrs. Sickles acted with "ordinary prudence." That may have been an understatement. Key had an apartment on 15th Street, just a block or so away, and they had a handkerchief-waving signal that had not escaped the notice of Washington gossips.

Theresa Sickles's happiness was short-lived. Someone slipped her husband an anonymous note telling him about "a guilty intrigue" between his wife and Key. It even named the rendezvous site. When Sickles confronted his wife with a charge of adultery, *Harper's* quotes her as saying, "Oh, I see I am discovered," and says she "implored her husband to spare her." Sickles did "spare" her—after she signed a confession in front of two witnesses. (It would be good evidence for a temporary insanity plea later.) By the next Sunday, Sickles was described as "totally distraught" in more than one account of the events of that day. "I am a dishonored and ruined man," he told a friend who paid him a visit. When Key walked past the Sickles house that morn-

ing, en route to the Washington Club, and allegedly signaled Theresa Sickles, it was the last straw. "I've seen the scoundrel making his signals," Sickles said to his friend, shaking his head and shouting, "My God, this is horrible."

Later, when he saw Key leave the Washington Club, Sickles rushed out into the square. As Key walked toward 16th Street, Sickles headed him off. "Key, you scoundrel, you have dishonored my house—you must die!" witnesses reported he shouted. Sickles fired one of his pistols. Almost at the same instant Key grabbed at his vest and lunged at Sickles, trying to prevent him from reloading. But Sickles stepped back into the middle of the street and produced another pistol. Key saw it and began backing up toward the Washington Club. Sickles stalked him. When he was ten feet away he fired, and as Key leaned against a tree pleading, "Don't shoot me," he fired once more.

As Key fell, his eyes moved once again toward that window across the square—the window he often used to watch through opera glasses from the Washington Club, according to *Harper's* Washington correspondent. Although he may have been looking for Theresa, it's likely that the last image his eyes registered was the smoking pistols of her vengeful husband. Within minutes there was an explosion of screams and sobs from the Sickles house. Theresa had learned what had happened.

The lifeless body of Key was removed and buried with proper respect. However, it is said that the spirit of the debonair lawyer has never left Lafayette Square. Stories of encounters with his persistent phantom have been handed down through the years. For one hundred years people have said they have seen Key. A few times newspapers have printed descriptions of Key's ghost as related to them by scores of eyewitnesses. Some have seen it walking out of the old Washington Club. Others claim to have encountered it on the sidewalk near where Key was slain. The Key spirit is also reported to have ventured into the square on occasion. According to the legend, it is that of a single-minded Key, intent upon keeping his rendezvous with his mistress.

The attitude that Daniel Sickles assumed toward his twenty-two-year-old wife "has gained him a great deal of sympathy," according to an article in *Harper's Weekly* shortly after the shooting. "He does not conceal his continued love for her; and while firmly insisting upon a divorce, he bestows upon her all the pity she needs." The trial was a spectacular one. Sickles hired the best lawyers money could buy, and was acquitted on the grounds of "temporary aberration of mind," used for the first time in this case. Some have claimed that the congressman's relationship with President Buchanan was well known to the jurors and intimated that the jury would not convict a man of such position and influence.

Although Sickles and his wife separated, his career did not falter. Theresa's life had ended with Key's death, and

Daniel Sickles as he appeared in later years, after he lost his leg in the Battle of Gettysburg. According to legend, he revisited the Army Medical Museum where the leg was on display until the museum moved to new quarters.

within a few years she too died. Sickles, however, continued his duties and attended to his social obligations as though nothing had ever happened. When the Civil War erupted, he raised his own contingent of men from New York and rode off into battle. His patriotism endeared him to President and Mrs. Abraham Lincoln, and assured him of a post after the war.

"He certainly is a very kind-hearted man," Mrs. Lincoln said of General Sickles, who sometimes dined at the White House. The loss of a leg in the battle at Gettysburg did not diminish the General's appeal to the opposite sex, nor did it slow him down in his career. Within a few years he successfully manipulated himself into a position to be named minister to Spain by President Ulysses S. Grant. Sickles is said to have worn his disability as a badge of courage. In fact, he thought so much of his severed leg that he personally bequeathed it to the Army's National Medical Museum.

Like Sickles the congressman, and Sickles the general, Sickles the diplomat possessed a tremendous ego. Legend has it that when he came back to Washington, he would often drop by the Medical Museum where his leg was "enshrined"— bringing a few friends with him. He loved pointing to the severed limb and retelling the tale of his valor when it was cut from under him.

After his death, his spirit is reported to have continued to visit the museum to admire the leg. A long-time custodian I met at the old Medical Museum of the Armed Forces Institute of Pathology wasn't at all reluctant to discuss Sickles's revisitations. The old man, bent with age, but sturdy enough to perform his tasks, claimed that his grandfather had served with Sickles in the Civil War. He took a rather curious pride in working around the leg, but seemed to wonder whether all the old stories about the General's ghost still visiting the museum would die out after the museum moved from the old red brick building in Southwest to the grounds of the Walter Reed Army Medical Center in Northwest. Although the custodian said he had never met the General's spirit, a coworker of his had.

Pointing to the hallway near the glass case containing the General's leg, the custodian told how the coworker had related his encounter with "a fat shadow with one leg that seemed to float" through the dimly lighted hallway. The custodian learned of the experience when the coworker came to him threatening to quit if he wasn't shifted to day work. The custodian said that he was sure the spirit the coworker had seen was Sickles's because there had been others over the years who had described similar encounters—always with a spirit they described as "obese," "fat," or "rotund" and with one leg.

The Hirshhorn Museum now occupies the spot where the old Medical Museum used to be, and none of its staff nor any of the visitors apparently has encountered the old General looking for his leg. And the ghost hasn't turned up at the new facilities at Walter Reed yet, either. Perhaps one day we will hear of him taking a group of spectral friends on a tour of the Hirshhorn.

SECRETARY WILLIAM SEWARD'S MEPHISTO SPIRIT

With the State Department next door to the White House during the Lincoln Administration, it seemed quite natural for Secretary of State William H. Seward to find a home near his work. He and his family chose a house on Lafayette Square that had been the quarters of the Washington Club, one of the city's most prominent gentleman's clubs, and that had also served as a house for such notables as Secretary of State Henry Clay and Vice President John C. Calhoun. It was outside this two-story brick home that Philip Barton Key's restless spirit was said to appear as he returned to keep his rendezvous with his mistress.

The Seward family, apparently untroubled by the ghost stories, settled in their new home in the early 1860's, at a time when the Civil War was drawing to a close and dissidents led by John Wilkes Booth were plotting a way to change Union policies. As part of this conspiracy, which resulted in the assassination of President Lincoln, Louis Powell, sometimes known as Paine, a former Confederate deserter and son of a Florida Baptist minister, was supposed to kill Seward. However, when he broke into the Seward house one night, Seward's son Frederick and a servant heard noises and surprised Powell before he could carry out his mission. One thing is certain, if help had not been summoned by the noises, Secretary Seward would have been killed. He was confined to his bed with injuries from a bad carriage accident, and could not defend himself against the attack. Fortunately, the others arrived at his bedside in time to save him from serious harm.

Who made the noises that brought help? That depends on what you read and whom you talk to. Some say Powell was clumsy; others insist Philip Barton Key's restless soul sensed another tragedy and made noise outside as Powell was breaking in.

The attempted assassination was such a shock to Seward's invalid wife that she died within two months, and his only daughter—who had witnessed the as-

46 sault, according to one newspaper account several years later—never recovered from the "horrendous experience" and died within a year. Seward gradually regained his health, and managed to overcome his great personal tragedies. He served under President Andrew Johnson for a time, but retired in 1869 and moved back to his home town of Auburn, New York. Within three years he too died.

Over the years, tales spread throughout the Lafayette Square neighborhood of a "Mephisto spirit" that haunted the former Seward house, making all sorts of noises and disrupting the households that lived there. Several owners tried to stick it out, including the YMCA, which occupied the house for a while during the 1880's. One newspaper article from that time questioned, "What revenant was roaming about? Had Key's spirit come in out of the damp and chilly night air?" Possibly, but all accounts of his spirit prior to then located him outside on the sidewalk or in the park, not inside. Some have speculated that the "Mephisto spirit" was Secretary Seward, frustrated in his attempts to reunite with his wife and daughter, who were also indirect victims of the Lincoln assassination conspiracy. Seward's spirit, certain mediums contended, could easily have traveled through the ether to revisit the place that had so dramatically affected his life.

Whatever the source, the restless spirit made life so miserable for anyone occupying the house that it apparently was difficult to find someone who would live there. In 1895 the house was torn down. Some feel that's exactly what the crafty old spirit wanted. After all, a spirit that had suffered as much as Seward's had could not be blamed for wanting the old house destroyed—his life certainly had been wrecked within its walls. Since the building was razed, the old "Mephisto spirit" has been dormant, and many hope it is a sign that Seward has found lasting peace.

Secretary William Seward's spirit is supposed to have haunted his old house on Lafayette Square, where he had known so much tragedy, until it was torn down. Only then did it find eternal rest.

THE RETURN OF THE TRAGIC MAJOR RATHBONE

Major Henry Rathbone, an unintentional victim of the Lincoln assassination, lost his sanity and took the life of his wife and then shot himself. Although the incident happened in Germany, people in Washington began avoiding his former home on Lafayette Square because they feared his spirit had returned, and would seek revenge.

The web that links families to a tragedy can be a strange one. Another former house on Lafayette Square belonged to still another victim of the Lincoln conspiracy. For years after the death of Major Henry Rathbone, people crossed the street rather than walk too close to his former Jackson Place residence.

Major Rathbone was a brilliant and successful young officer when he moved into Number 8 Jackson Place. At that time he was hopeful of making New York Senator Harris's daughter Clara his wife. It was Miss Harris who accompanied the Major the night he went with President and Mrs. Lincoln to see *Our American Cousin* at Ford's Theatre. Major Rathbone was stabbed in the head and neck by John Wilkes Booth before the assassin made good his escape by jumping onto the stage from the presidential box.

Although seriously wounded, Major Rathbone responded to treatment and physically recovered from his wounds, but his mind was never quite the same. He was distracted, moody. He and Clara Harris were eventually married, and his wife accepted his moods, thinking that some day he would again become the man she used to know. Perhaps that is why she agreed to move with him to Germany.

Hoping to escape his recurring depression, the Major resigned his commission and with his wife set out for Hanover. Another country and another life, however, proved no panacea. He became even more despondent. As his wife and children prepared for the coming Christmas holidays, Rathbone seemed to lose touch with reality altogether. He took a gun, shot his wife to death, and would have killed his children if a nurse had not intervened. He then shot himself. Whether or not Rathbone was reliving that struggle some eighteen years earlier with John Wilkes Booth is only conjecture.

Doctors were able to save what was left of the life of Henry Rathbone, but he spent the rest of his days in an insane asylum far from his former home on Lafayette Square.

The news of the Rathbone tragedy quickly reached Washington. Some of his former neighbors wept at the misfortune, but as they walked along Jackson Place they often took their children by the hand and crossed over into the park rather than walk directly in front of the old Rathbone house. They seemed to be afraid the web of fate that had entangled so many victims of the Lincoln assassination might still hang in the air around the house of the unfortunate Major. A few expressed fear that his deranged spirit would cross the ocean, while others contended it already had. They whispered of hearing a man crying. Tales spun over backyard fences or on porches at night told of heartbreaking sobs drifting from the old home where, for a few brief years Rathbone had known success, joy, and happiness.

Clara Harris Rathbone was with Henry Rathbone at Ford's Theatre the night of the Lincoln assassination, a night from which he never recovered.

THE GRIEF OF MARIAN ADAMS

Sequestered among holly bushes and ivy in the old Rock Creek Cemetery off North Capitol Street in upper Northwest Washington is the grave of Marian Hooper Adams. It bears no inscription. It bears no date. Marking the grave is the Augustus Saint-Gaudens statue commissioned by her husband, historian Henry Adams.

Many who have seen the figure have felt compelled to call it "Grief," although Adams himself never liked that name.

The "poor, unfortunate Mrs. Adams," as neighbors referred to her after her untimely death, may have been unfortunate, but she was not poor. She was intelligent, well educated, and beautiful. The Adamses lived across from St. John's Church on H Street, Northwest. The Hay-Adams Hotel occupies the site now. Prior to settling in Washington, Adams had been an assistant professor of history at Harvard. Some neighbors who thought the Adamses had a well-adjusted and intellectually compatible marital relationship, were surprised at the circumstances surrounding Marian's death.

During the last years of their marriage, Marian Adams became ill. Henry had his work, and some articles of the period said he continued to travel a good deal while his invalid wife remained at home. Although there was no outward sign of disenchantment with such an arrangement, some conjectured later that there was inner conflict. Adams returned home one cold winter's evening to find his wife lying unconscious before the fire. She never revived. Adams was quoted in one newspaper of the day as saying he knew his wife's health had been improving, because only that morning she had expressed much optimism over her condition. He said nothing more, declining thereafter to discuss the death with anyone. The attempt by one so influential and famous as Henry Adams to keep the circumstances surrounding the death of his wife quiet had the opposite effect. Rumors spread. Suicide? Murder? Questions multiplied and speculation abounded. What could have caused Marian Adams's death? Few believed it had been the state of her health, so they talked even more after the story began to circulate that she had taken her own life. They blamed Henry for leaving her alone so much of the time while he traveled around the world. Unable to understand his work or his life-style, they labeled him eccentric.

Adams himself did much after his wife's death to perpetuate the belief in his eccentricity. When he chose Washington's oldest cemetery as the resting place for his wife, he ordered that no stone, nor marker of any kind, be placed on the grave. He commissioned Augustus Saint-Gaudens to create a monument in bronze, but instructed the sculptor that "no . . . attempt is to be made to make it intelligible to the average mind."

While the statue was being readied, the historian shrugged off the barbs of neighbors and continued his work. He devoted himself almost entirely to his historical research and writings, and traveled extensively. The house was dark a great deal of the time, which added to the mystery that was beginning to build up around it. Stories spread that "visitors to the house were overcome with uneasiness and would not remain for long." It was said that occasionally, at dusk, the sighs and bitter sobs of a woman crying could be heard from within. There were tales that the house was never warm, that in spite of the hottest of fires there was always a chill around the hearth—where Marian was found unconscious.

The ghost in the Adams house began to receive a great deal of attention in newspapers within ten years of Marian Adams's death. An article that seemed to have been written around the turn of the century (there was no date or credit on the clipping I saw in the files of the Washingtoniana section of the D.C. Public Library), related several incidents that had occurred over a period of a few years. There were those who had been awakened in the night by sounds of gentle rocking. Some related encounters with the spirit of a sad-eyed lady "who sits and rocks in a large oak chair" that is as shadowy as she. The woman's unblinking eyes stare directly into the eyes of the person before whom she has appeared.

Those who had such an encounter said they were compelled to stare back but that their initial fears seemed to vanish as they were overtaken by the deep feeling of loneliness and despair generated by the apparition. It is said that some broke into uncontrollable sobbing, and then took weeks to regain their composure. It is as though the woman could transfer her emotions, although she never moved from the rocking chair. Always seen in a bedroom of the house—Marian's room—the shade would sit and rock and stare with never a change of expression until a loud scream, or a frantic motion, caused it to vanish. The events detailed in this particular article bear a strong similarity to the legend handed down by word of mouth about the statue erected by Henry Adams at his wife's grave in Rock Creek Cemetery.

When Saint-Gaudens completed the work he had been commissioned to create, and Adams tried to have it placed in the cemetery, he met resistance. Cemetery officials took one look at the statue and said no. They felt it was not a fitting memorial, but the persistent Adams insisted on installing it, and won. Adams —who made no mention of his wife in his autobiography—saw to it that the statue bore no inscription either. It is said that he once referred to it as "The Peace of God," but didn't like people calling it "Grief." Many of those who have visited Rock Creek Cemetery and stood before the statue have said that there is no way to express, or measure, the coldness that enveloped them as they looked upon "Grief." It is described by some as a feeling of "extreme loneliness." Others spoke of being overcome by a tremendous sadness and a feeling of despair like none they had ever known.

A cemetery groundskeeper recalled how some who have sat alone in front of the statue, which is surrounded by a brooding grove of holly trees, have related that the weathered bronzed eyes seemed to come to life. They say the pupils stare back from the shadows of the greenish oxidized cowl that overhangs the forehead and sides of the face.

Another legend told by some is that people who have meditated there have sometimes been joined, at dusk, by the ethereal form of a beautiful but frail

woman dressed in the clothing of the late 1880's. Some say it is the reverberations of her despair that permeate the holly grove, compelling all those who look upon Saint-Gaudens's statue to call it "Grief."

Those who visit the statue that marks the grave of Marian Adams in Rock Creek Cemetery have felt compelled to call it "Grief."
Some have said that they have encountered a presence that brings with it a feeling of almost unbearable despair and sorrow.

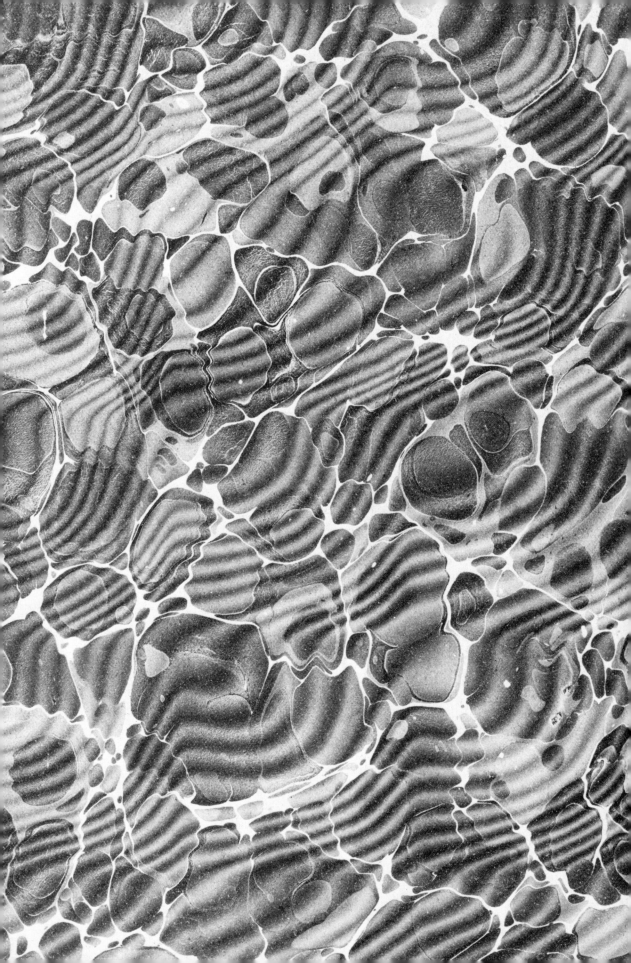

3. THE WHITE HOUSE

ABIGAIL ADAMS AND HER LAUNDRY

George Washington never lived in the White House, though he was instrumental in choosing its location. His first presidential residence was in New York, his next one in Philadelphia.

The first family to occupy the President's House was not unlike any other family that has to move into a new home that isn't completed. John and Abigail Adams had to tolerate all the inconvenience inside, plus a wide, muddy, and unpaved Pennsylvania Avenue. Abigail used to say that even though the East Room wasn't completed, it was the dryest area in the house. That's the room she used to hang her wash in.

Tricia Nixon Cox, daughter of the thirty-seventh President, said at one time that she was fascinated by the history of the East Room, which included not only affairs of state, but a few weddings and even the quartering of troops. Tricia smiled as she recalled the stories about Mrs. Adams's washdays but said that she

The Adamses, the first First Family to occupy the President's House, moved in before it was completed. Even today, the spirit of Abigail Adams is supposed to carry loads of laundry to hang in the East Room.

personally had not encountered Abigail wandering through those East Room doors. Over the years, though, there have been those who have seen Mrs. Adams, with arms outstretched as though carrying a load of laundry. Her spirit passes through the locked doors to the East Room, where she spent many hours during her husband's Presidency. Some say that they can tell when Abigail's spirit has been there, for it leaves behind the faint smell of soap and damp clothing.

The White House seems to lend itself to ghost stories. Liz Carpenter, press secretary to Lady Bird Johnson, described it as "a house forever changing, yet always the same." It has been rebuilt a number of times. After the British put the torch to it in the War of 1812, there was even talk of relocating the government. The rains that fell on the city the night of the fire, however, extinguished the blaze and left enough brick and mortar standing to make rebuilding feasible. The foundation and walls were made sound once again, and were repainted to cover the effects of the fire. Although the President's House had always been white, and might have been called the White House before, after this the name stuck permanently.

JAMES A. GARFIELD'S PSYCHIC POWERS

President James A. Garfield had only four months in the White House before a disappointed office seeker, Charles J. Guiteau, wounded him at Union Station. The bullet, which entered Garfield's back, eventually killed him, though some specialists today think that if the doctors had left the bullet alone, Garfield probably would have lived. What the doctors could not have known then was that the bullet had lodged in his back muscles only inches from the point of entry. It was harmless, but infection from the unsterile instruments wasn't. Seventy-nine days after he had been wounded, James Garfield was dead.

Garfield had been a deeply religious man. In addition to theology, his studies included biology and anthropology. Just what psychic powers Garfield possessed can only be speculated on, but he confided to close friends that he had seen and conversed with the spirit of his departed father on several occasions, including at least one contact while he was in the White House.

Above: This painting from Library of Congress collection is entitled: "A view of the Presidents House in the City of Washington after the Conflagration of the 24th August 1814."

Below: President James A. Garfield had psychic powers, and claimed that he was visited in the White House by the spirit of his long-dead father.

Then there's the ghost of a British soldier from the War of 1812, who is supposed to have died on the White House grounds, that still haunts the house once in a while. Generally, he is reported with a torch in hand. His most recent appearance was recorded in a 1954 *Washington Star* article. Leslie Lieber told how a former valet for the President recalled one occasion when he was packing luggage for a visiting couple who were obviously very upset. The woman appeared nervous and the man seemed irritable as he told the valet: "Somebody, my wife insists it was a ghost, was trying to set fire to our beds all night long."

DEPARTED VISITORS OF THE ROSE ROOM

One spot in the White House that seems to be frequented by a ghost or ghosts is the Rose Room, often called the Queen's Bedroom because five queens have stayed there. With its adjacent dressing room and bath, it makes a comfortable apartment. The bed, which probably belonged to Andrew Jackson, has been the source of ribald laughter for more than a century. More than one person is said to have heard the sounds, and often their tales have been repeated in newspapers.

Storytellers like to recall the scandal involving Jackson and Peggy O'Neil. The beautiful, vivacious daughter of a Washington tavern keeper used to entertain Jackson and a friend of his, John Eaton, at her father's tavern. Her jealous husband apparently couldn't stand it. Rumor has it that he took his own life. The recently widowed Jackson liked Peggy a lot, but he also felt certain presidential responsibilities. He encouraged Eaton to marry the girl, and when Eaton did, Jackson appointed Eaton to his Cabinet as a wedding present.

The appointment caused quite a stir, and the Cabinet wives snubbed the witty Peggy Eaton because they didn't approve

56 of her morals. Secretary of State Martin Van Buren liked her, though. His attention to the "beautiful Mrs. Eaton was obvious"—to quote one ancient article. The scandal was too much. Jackson accepted Eaton's "resignation" and then sent Peggy and her husband to Spain in an attempt to quiet the gossips.

Liz Carpenter, who was closely associated with the White House during the Johnson Administration, referred to the old story of invisible laughter coming from Jackson's bed, and said with a twinkle in her eye, "He was such a salty old character, I've often wondered if it was his laugh."

Death had come to Old Hickory in 1845 at his Nashville estate, The Hermitage. Within twenty years, however, his spirit was first reported revisiting the White House by none other than Mary Todd Lincoln. The mystical Mrs. Lincoln told friends that she often heard Jackson stomping and swearing.

A White House staff member, Lillian Rogers Parks, in a 1961 book, *My 30 Years Backstairs at the White House,* tells of experiencing what she believed was an actual encounter with Jackson in the Rose Room. She was busily hemming a bedspread in preparation for a visit from Queen Elizabeth II when she felt a presence in the room.

The air directly behind her seemed cold as she sensed someone looking over her shoulder. She could feel a hand on the back of her chair. Her scalp tightened, but fear would not let her look around. Leaving behind her sewing basket and needle and thread, the seamstress quickly left, and it was weeks before anyone could talk her into going back in there. When she did have to return to the room, she said that she made certain she never went alone.

The bed in the Rose Room is supposed to be the one used by Andrew Jackson. Ribald laughter attributed to his ghost is sometimes heard coming from it. It was also in the Rose Room that the ghost of Abraham Lincoln appeared before Queen Wilhelmina of the Netherlands several decades ago.

DEPARTED VISITORS OF THE YELLOW OVAL ROOM

The Yellow Oval Room has one of the most magnificent views in all of Washington. Looking out toward the Mall, one can see the tall spire of the Washington Monument, the majestic Lincoln Memorial, and across the Tidal Basin and through the Japanese cherry trees, the dome of the Jefferson Memorial.

Thomas Jefferson used the room as a drawing room, and often relaxed by playing his violin there. "My, my," Mary Todd Lincoln once said to a friend, "how that Mr. Jefferson does play the violin." Jefferson had been dead a number of years before Mary Lincoln and her husband moved into the White House. I read in the *Washington Daily News* that she also told some of her closest friends just after John Tyler died in 1862 that she sometimes heard his spirit returning to the Oval Room to woo his twenty-year-old wife.

It is also in that room that Woodrow Wilson proposed to the second Mrs. Wilson; and that Franklin Roosevelt re-

The Yellow Oval Room has had its share of spectral visitors including Thomas Jefferson and John Tyler.

Byrnes was upstairs playing a trick on him, the guard rushed to the attic stairs, but found the entrance sealed. The guard told the reporter that he later learned the Secretary had not even been in the White House that day.

The reporter nodded understandingly, shrugged his shoulders, and left. He marked it off as idle conversation until a week or so later when the reporter read something that caused him to change that assessment. It was an article about White House land acquisition. The hairs on the back of his neck bristled and his flesh tingled as he recalled the guard's story. He stared at the name of the man who had owned the land in 1790. His name was David Burns, dubbed "Obstinate Davy" by President Washington because he had not wanted to sell the land.

THE EVER-PRESENT MR. LINCOLN

Lincoln was fifty-two when he came into the White House, and there were almost as many Presidents before him as have followed him. None has left the mark on the executive mansion that he has. Indeed, many swear that his spirit still walks the halls. More than a few have testified to having seen his form standing at the center window of the Oval Room. During the Civil War he is said to have often stood there—looking out at Virginia with silent concern about the fate of the Union and the miseries of war.

Lincoln undoubtedly possessed some psychic gifts. Scholars have described him as "introspective," and some said that his periods of silence were trance-like. As a child and a teen-ager, Lincoln was said to have been somewhat moody, yet he always attracted friends.

His personal life was often touched by tragedy. He lost his deeply religious mother when he was four. When his first love, Ann Rutledge, died of typhoid, the

ceived the leaders of Congress the day after Pearl Harbor. Noted Lincoln scholar Carl Sandburg spent quite some time meditating in the room a few years ago, then emerged convinced that it was the room in which Lincoln had reached most of his great decisions.

During the Truman years, a White House guard related to a reporter that he had heard a voice calling out to him—seemingly from the attic above the Yellow Oval Room. In a whisper, the voice said: "I'm Mr. Burns. I'm Mr. Burns."

Thinking Secretary of State James

Mary and Abraham Lincoln with their sons (from left to right) Willie, who died during his father's presidency, Tad, and Robert.

trauma thrust him into a profound melancholy, which apparently led to an emotional breakdown several years later.

In 1842 Lincoln married Mary Todd. They had an indisputably rocky marriage. Some have said that it was held together only by their common love for their children. Of those children, only Robert became an adult. Edward died at age four, Willie died of fever in the middle of his father's first term as President, and Tad outlived his father by only six years.

Willie possibly was his father's favorite, and the little boy's unexpected death had a profound impact not only on the President, but on Mary Lincoln as well. The family had no gravesite in Washington, but Supreme Court Clerk William Thomas Carroll offered Lincoln a tomb for his son in the Carroll family tomb in Oak Hill Cemetery.

Lincoln used to spend long hours at that crypt, which is on a narrow path on a hillside overlooking Rock Creek. There are two wrought iron chairs behind the locked iron gates of the crypt, giving credence to the old newspaper reports that on at least two occasions Lincoln had the crypt opened so that he could look at his son. Legend has it that he would sit and stare at the dead youth for hours and weep. Lincoln could not bear to leave Willie alone in that cold, dank, dark tomb.

Members of President Ulysses S. Grant's household believed in the ability to communicate with the dead, and one of them is reported to have conversed with Willie's spirit. More recently, Lynda Johnson Robb, who occupied the room in which Willie died, was "very much" aware of the fact that "it was in her room the little Lincoln boy breathed his last breath," Liz Carpenter told me, but declined to elaborate.

Willie Lincoln died at the age of 12 during his father's presidency and was buried in the Carroll family tomb in Oak Hill Cemetery. Lincoln is supposed to have sat in this chair looking at the crypt and weeping. Willie's ghost has been seen around the White House on several occasions.

She also said that Lady Bird Johnson encountered what she believed was Lincoln's presence one April evening as she watched a television special on Lincoln's death. "Suddenly, she was aware, conscious of the fact, that the room she was in was special." Someone was compelling her to direct her eyes toward the mantel." It wasn't the mantel that her eyes focused on, however, but a small plaque she had never noticed before. Liz Carpenter said that it told of the room's importance to Lincoln, and that as Lady Bird Johnson read it, she felt "a chill. A draft." Mrs. Carpenter recalled that Mrs. Johnson told her later that she felt very ill at ease. "Perhaps she felt his presence."

Lincoln was not much for organized religion, though on occasion he would attend Presbyterian services. As a politician his views on religion had been questioned, and once when he was running for Congress he distributed a handbill denying that he had ever spoken "with intentional disrespect of religion." Lincoln did seem to be at least curious about spiritualism. His wife's pursuit of the supernatural was more overt, especially after Willie's death. She frequently consulted spiritualists and mediums, and there is even a photograph of Mary Todd Lincoln seated at a table with a ghostlike Abraham superimposed behind her. It is thought to be the work of a spiritualist photographer in the 1870's.

Séances were held at the White House, and there are newspaper records to indicate that Abraham Lincoln attended a couple of these. The *Chicago Tribune* reported in 1863 that medium Charles Shockle visited the White House. The levitation and rapping that the President witnessed seemed to impress him. In 1967, Suzy Smith wrote in *Prominent American Ghosts* that she had learned of another time when a medium visited the President. A skeptical Lincoln is said to have ordered a congressman from Maine to sit on top of a piano that a medium

was successfully levitating. The congress-man's weight made no difference. President and congressman and others watching could hardly believe their eyes as the piano and the congressman rose and fell at the medium's command.

A *National Geographic News Bulletin* from August 1973 heralding a Library of Congress exhibit on spiritualism, recalled that the medium J. B. Conklin supposedly received a telepathic message from Edward D. Baker for President Lincoln, who was a close friend of Baker's. Conklin received his message for the President two months after Baker had been killed leading Union forces into action at Ball's Bluff, Virginia. Conklin told him Baker's message was "gone elsewhere" and that "elsewhere is everywhere."

Many of the occupants of the White House seem to have been visited by Lincoln. "I think of Lincoln, shambling, homely, with his sad, strong, deeply furrowed face, all the time," said President Theodore Roosevelt. "I see him in the different rooms and in the halls," he admitted some forty years after Lincoln's occupancy.

Grace Coolidge is said to have seen the specter of the President, too. In a newspaper account I read, she said that he was dressed "in black, with a stole draped across his shoulders to ward off the drafts and chills of Washington's night air."

President Dwight Eisenhower's press secretary, James Haggerty, once said on an ABC-TV news program that the President had told him he often felt Lincoln's presence. President Harry Truman recalled that in the early morning hours a little over a year after he became President, he was awakened by two distinct knocks on the door of his bedroom. He got up and went to the door, opened it, but found no one in the hall. Just a cold spot that went away as footsteps trailed off down the corridor. Truman wrote in

The Lincoln Bedroom as it looked around the turn of the century. Lincoln has been seen most often in this room, although his spirit is said to wander through most of the White House.

his diary that he wished he had the bravado to summon forth the Lincoln ghost to scare his daughter and a friend who were spending a night in the Lincoln bedroom.

Eleanor Roosevelt denied to reporters that she personally had seen Lincoln's apparition, but she did admit to feeling his presence. She also related a story involving one of her staffers who had an encounter. Her secretary had passed Lincoln's bedroom one day and saw a lanky figure sitting on the bed pulling on his boots. Since Lincoln had been dead more than three-quarters of a century, the girl felt justified in her reaction: she screamed and ran as fast as her legs would carry her from the second floor. An article in the *Washington Star* said on another occasion that FDR's valet ran screaming from the White House and into the arms of a guard, shouting that he had just seen Lincoln.

Visitors also have encountered Lincoln's ghost. When Queen Wilhelmina of the Netherlands was visiting the White House quite a few years ago, she is supposed to have heard a knock on the door of the Rose Room, where she was staying. The hour was late, but thinking it could be important, she opened the door. Standing before the Queen, his large frame taking up most of the doorway, was Abraham Lincoln. A White House staffer said that the Queen shocked the President and other guests when she related the incident at cocktails the next evening. She told them that when she saw the chilling apparition everything went black, and when she came to, she was lying on the floor.

Winston Churchill never discussed it, but he did not like to sleep in the Lincoln bedroom. It is the room that all visiting male heads of state are quartered in, but the British Prime Minister was quite uncomfortable there. Often Churchill would be found across the hall the next morning. Susan Ford, daughter of President Gerald Ford, shares the uneasiness Churchill felt. She declared in *Seventeen* Magazine in the summer of 1975 that she believes in ghosts and has no intention of ever sleeping in the Lincoln bedroom.

Lincoln spent many restless nights in

President Lincoln's body lay in state in the East Room after his assassination, just as he had dreamed it would.

that massive old room, and no doubt suffered through more nightmares than pleasant dreams. *Encyclopaedia Britannica* says that Lincoln believed in dreams and "other enigmatic signs and portents" throughout his life. Several of his dreams have been reported, but none is more memorable than Lincoln's vision of his own death. The President recalled one of his dreams in which he had heard weeping, sobbing, and wailing. Walking down a White House corridor to investigate, the President said that he saw a coffin lying in state. Inquiring from a mourner, "Who is dead?" Lincoln was told, "The assassinated President." Lincoln said that in his dream, he walked over to the coffin and looking inside, saw himself.

April 14, 1865, had begun rather routinely for President Lincoln. During the morning, and for part of the afternoon, he met with Cabinet officials to map Re-

The phantom of Mary Surratt's daughter, Anna, has been seen knocking at the White House door, still pleading for the release of her mother.

construction plans. Later that day, he and Mrs. Lincoln went for a carriage ride. They returned home late in the afternoon to dress for the theater. Often,

going to the theater or opera took the President's mind off his troubles. General and Mrs. Ulysses S. Grant had been unable to accompany the President and Mrs. Lincoln to Ford's that night, but Major Henry Rathbone and Clara Harris had accepted the President's invitation. The rest of the story has been retold many times. By the next morning Lincoln was dead, the victim of an assassin's bullet.

The prosecution of the conspirators was vigorously pursued, and feeling ran high about exacting retribution. There is some question even today, however, about the guilt of at least one of those convicted of conspiring to assassinate the President. Some believe that Mary Surratt was unjustly punished. On the eve of her execution, her daughter Anna forced her way inside the White House grounds and made it to the front door, where she pleaded for her mother's release. On the anniversary of that night, some have claimed to have seen Anna's spirit banging on the front door of the White House, pleading once more for her mother's release.

It has been well over one hundred years since Lincoln's death, but based on the stories of scores of responsible White House employees, members of presidential families, and Presidents themselves, the spirit of that great American still roams the hallways, still cares about the nation he fought so mightily to preserve. Although there have been several who have run screaming from the Lincoln ghost, there are others, particularly those whose turn it is to make decisions of state, who do not fear it. His presence seems to offer comfort and strength to them.

"Why would they want to come back here I could never understand," Harry Truman is quoted as having said about the White House ghosts. In her book *Harry S. Truman,* daughter Margaret says that her father was sure ghosts were in the White House, and at one time he wrote ". . . so I won't lock my doors or bar them either. . . ."

Truman himself had no ambition to haunt the White House, he wrote in a letter to daughter Margaret: "No man in his right mind would want to come here of his own accord."

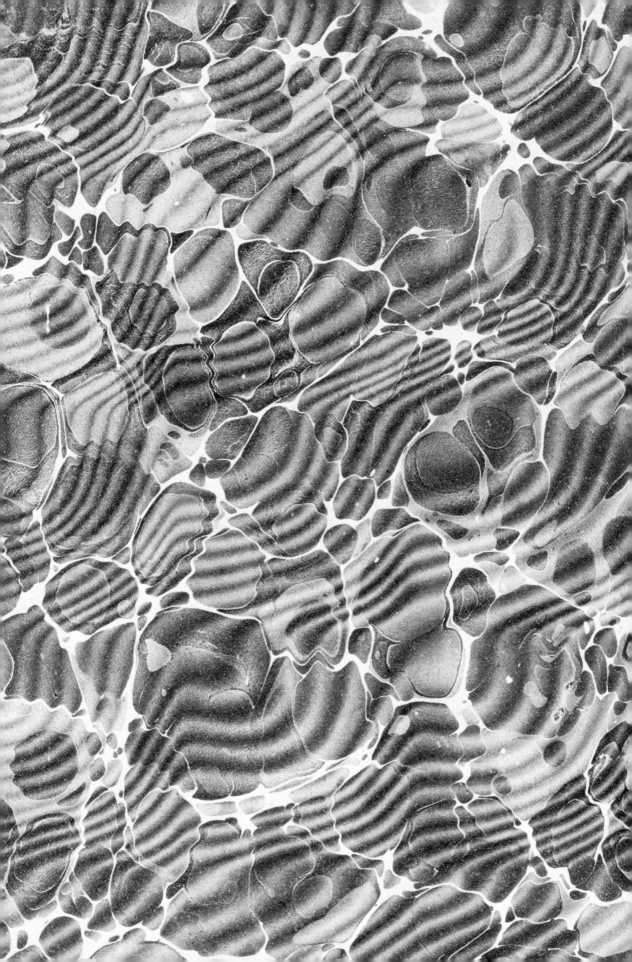

4.THE CAPITOL

George Washington, first President of the United States, laid the cornerstone of the U.S. Capitol building in 1793. Seven years later when the first section of the building was completed, Congress moved from its temporary headquarters in Philadelphia to the District of Columbia. The Capitol has undergone seven expansions since then, which have proliferated its narrow marble halls, winding passageways, dank, dark basements, dimly lighted corridors, and infinite rooms and subbasements. Almost from the beginning, the building became the object of a multitude of stories—not at all political in nature.

THE WORKERS WHO NEVER LEAVE

One of the earliest spirits reported to be roaming the Capitol corridors belonged to a stonemason who had somehow been sealed into one of the walls while the building was under construction. It is said that the man has been seen—trowel in hand—passing through a wall in the basement on the Senate side of the building. Some say the mason had the misfortune to lose an argument to a hotheaded carpenter who smashed in his head with a brick and used the man's own trowel to seal his tomb.

Down through the years quite a few people have sworn that they have seen the silent specter of a workman who fell from the giant Rotunda scaffolding, gliding through a hallway. On the anniversary of his fall, the worker, clad in his faded overalls and carrying his wooden tool kit, retraces his journey through the hallway en route to the Rotunda.

There is a story told by some of the cleaning crew who used to scrub the

This photograph of the Capitol was taken in the 1860's around the time that the first encounters with the ghost of a workman killed in a fall from the Rotunda scaffolding occurred. Newspapers have chronicled his appearance many times since.

marble floors of the mammoth building. One of their colleagues collapsed and died one evening with his scrub brush in his hand. They found his body the next morning slumped over the water pail. Legend has it that when the hour grows late and all but the maintenance staff and guards have gone home, water sloshing from an imaginary pail and the sound of incessant scrubbing is often heard.

JOHN Q. ADAMS'S ETERNAL SPEECH

Before the House and Senate wings were added, the House of Representatives chamber was in what is now Statuary Hall. Although the hall is dark at night, and the statues of the states' favorite sons are barely distinguishable, some say they have had little trouble seeing an "illuminated transparency" that closely resembles John Quincy Adams. After his term as President of the United States, Adams ran for Congress because he felt he still had much to contribute to the new country. So did his constituents. They elected the former President to nine terms as their representative in the Congress. Among his colleagues in the House he was known as "the Old Man Eloquent," and raised his voice in opposition to slavery and to the administration's war with Mexico. Adams was eighty-one years old when he stood up once more on February 23, 1848, to speak out against the majority. The Mexican War was over, and in celebration of victory Congress wanted to bestow special honors on the generals who had won it for them. Adams never finished his speech about what he considered "a most unrighteous war with Mexico." He suffered a cerebral stroke, fell unconscious onto the House floor, and had to be carried into the Speaker's office. There he died two days later.

A few years after his death, some of the Capitol workers began telling of colleagues who had seen Adams's ghost revisiting the House chamber. Accounts of

John Quincy Adams seems to have been unable to stop making speeches. Even though he was fatally stricken in the middle of a speech on the floor of the House, he still returns on certain evenings to make speeches in the old House chamber.

eyewitnesses to this occurrence are chronicled in several newspaper articles spanning a century. Those quoted refer to a "figure that appears to be delivering a speech." The place of the encounter is always on the spot where "the Old Man Eloquent" was fatally stricken.

THE NEW YEAR'S EVE PARTY IN STATUARY HALL

The 1840 House of Representatives was the last to hold sessions in the old House chamber before it became Statuary Hall. In the 1890's one old Capitol guard swore that he stumbled into the old chamber late one night and interrupted the entire membership in ghostly assembly. The writer of the article also indicated that he might have had a half pint in his pocket that night. In spite of ridicule, the old guard stuck to his story.

It is said that at midnight on New Year's Eve the statues here in Statuary Hall come down off their pedestals and dance with one another to celebrate another year of survival for the Republic.

And his tale has been told time and again by those who have worked in the Capitol.

My favorite tale about Statuary Hall involved a crusty old guard whose name has not been recorded for posterity but who is remembered, nevertheless, for what he saw. It seems that the old fellow began to develop considerable apprehension as the various statues were being placed on their pedestals in the old House chamber. The life-size figures were just *too* lifelike. While others around the Capitol expressed fears that the weight of the statues might cause the floor to give way, the old guard was more concerned with the statues themselves. He was uneasy around them.

One New Year's Eve, as he ap-proached the hall, he was stopped dead in his tracks. In the distance, a clock was striking twelve, and down the corridor in the room washed with soft light, he clearly saw silhouettes float down off pedestals. By his account to a reporter shortly after the incident, "Grant shook hands with Lee."

The guard opened his mouth but could not summon a scream. He was pet-rified with fear. Where had the light come from? What had illuminated "those marble manes," as the newspaper article put it. As the reverberation of the clock's last chime died away, the guard rubbed his eyes, but the vision was not gone. The figures began to dance. There in Statuary Hall in the stillness of a New Year's midnight, he looked upon a scene to rival any ever witnessed before, or ap-parently since: statues had come to life and were dancing. Quivering with fright the guard fled the Capitol.

The old man just couldn't keep quiet about what he had seen. In the light of

According to legend, the Unknown Soldier whose casket is here being decorated by President Harding revisits the Rotunda whenever a famous American lies in state there. Witnesses claim that the specter snaps a brisk salute and then vanishes.

the next day, although still trembling and blanched with fear, he told of his nightmare. Well, the story was just too much for the head of the Capitol Police, who prescribed a long, long rest for the guard. Since then, others have reported similar experiences, and, even today, some guards as they make their rounds try to avoid Statuary Hall at midnight, especially on New Year's Eve.

A DOUGHBOY'S SALUTE

Many other spirits are said to revisit the Capitol building. Legend has it that whenever a fallen soldier is laid in state in the huge Rotunda, a transparent doughboy makes himself visible momentarily—just long enough to snap a crisp salute. Some people think the doughboy may be the spirit of the World War One soldier who lay there before being placed in the Tomb of the Unknown Soldier in Arlington National Cemetery.

FISHBAIT MILLER'S CHICKEN GHOSTS

William "Fishbait" Miller has been around the Capitol for more than half of his life. While he was still the House doorkeeper, he told me: "Sometimes you sit here and think you hear the funniest things a' going on. You really wonder if you are still here—or what." Among the "queer noises" Miller says he has been unable to pinpoint are "those infernal clucking sounds."

The spirit of General John Alexander Logan has been reported listening outside the room where the Military Affairs Committee, which he once headed, is meeting. It has also been seen wandering in darkened basement corridors in search of his horse, which had been stuffed and placed on display, and then inadvertently sealed in a basement room.

I couldn't tell whether he was serious, or just trying to lead me down one of those narrow, winding Capitol corridors. His face expressed bewilderment as he spoke of the puzzling sounds he said he has often heard. Then his face erupted into a broad grin as he recalled how one old congressman in bygone days used to bring chickens into the Capitol with him. "Wonder," Miller said, "if those sounds I keep a'hearin' are chicken ghosts?"

As for other tales, Miller would not say whether he believed all the old stories he has heard down through the years. Most of the legends about the ghosts in the Capitol have been spun by those who have spent considerable time within its hallways and rooms. But there are some apparitions that are said to have made themselves visible not only to Capitol staffers, but to visitors too.

GENERAL LOGAN'S CONSTANT CONCERN

General John Alexander Logan, who gained fame in the Mexican and Civil wars, was a violent partisan, and identified with the radical wing of the Republican party. The General served in both the House and Senate during his Capitol Hill career. Some visitors who have walked past the old room where the Committee on Military Affairs used to meet, claim to have spotted the old General. He has been dead quite a few years, so their shock is understandable. It is said that the General still wears his famous slouch hat, but his face is marked with "deep concern" as he listens in the corridor. Apparently, the General, who presided over the committee almost one hundred years ago, isn't too happy with the way things have been run in his absence.

THE RETURN OF GARFIELD AND HIS ASSASSIN

A few years after the death of President James Garfield, a newspaper article about ghosts in the Capitol said that the assassinated President had been seen silently walking the Capitol halls while his body was lying in state. Even his politically ambitious assailant, Charles Guiteau, was spotted in the Capitol. A guard testified to the reporter that he had encountered the assassin on a stairway leading into the Capitol basement. The guard said that he had started to give chase thinking Guiteau had escaped, but as he suddenly remembered that the execution had taken place the previous week, the figure vanished.

UNCLE JOE CANNON AND CHAMP CLARK

The staccato rap of a gavel on the House Speaker's dais is not an uncommon sound when Congress is in session. But during the late night hours it can only mean a revisit from Uncle Joe Cannon and Champ Clark. The conjecture is that these former House Speakers keep returning to re-enact their famous confrontation.

The conservative Cannon and the progressive Clark squared off in 1910 when Clark, as Democratic floor leader, led his party in revolt against "Cannonism." Both men spent most of their lives in the House, and each served as Speaker for eight years. Guards who have reported seeing the phantoms of the former Speakers revisiting the scene of many of their battles, say they always come at night, and the chamber is always pitch-black.

The ghosts of Champ Clark (left) and Joe Cannon, former Speakers of the House of Representatives, are among those who return to the Capitol from time to time to continue their earthly debates.

Former House doorkeeper William "Fishbait" Miller said that during one late-night House session sounds reverberating down Capitol hallways became so bothersome that he ordered the doors to the chamber bolted so that lawmakers would not be distracted from their work.

THE INVISIBLE GUARD

Late at night the sounds of footsteps made by invisible visitors sometimes trail guards down dimly-lighted corridors like this one.

Tales are told of elusive footsteps heard in empty Capitol corridors. A nonbelieving guard was determined to prove that they were simply an echo. Wearing rubber-soled shoes, he set out on his rounds one night determined not to make noise. As he walked, he smiled at the silence. The guard enjoyed an inner sense of accomplishment, thinking how he could boast to his colleagues in the morning of having personally bested one of the Capitol's so-called ghosts.

His smirk was short-lived. The silence was broken by approaching footsteps. His immediate thought was that a fellow worker was catching up to him and he would be able to share his success. The smile on his lips faded, however, because when he turned around, the hallway was deserted.

The footsteps seemed to move closer, yet the guard saw no one. The guard now tried to convince himself that someone was playing a joke on him. A good way to prove it would be to corner the footsteps, he thought. So he resumed walking. The guard entered the next office, hoping the culprit would fall into his trap. But when he turned to confront the practical joker, no one was there. The only sound to be heard was his own heavy breathing. Then, faintly, from another hallway, he heard footsteps. The sound came from the other side of the office wall. How did they get over there? How did the elusive footsteps pass silently through the office wall?

The old guard could never explain it. Many have tried, including some who had similar experiences. Other guards have said that they too have had "sensations of being followed" and "heard noises." Some describe "sounds like footsteps" that sometimes tailed them through the lonely corridors. However, only a few have expressed fear. Most feel that the footsteps are probably those of some ancient Capitol guard who was so dedicated to his job that he still visits from time to time to walk his appointed rounds.

Vice President Henry Wilson loved to "tub" in the Senate basement until he caught a congestive chill and died. Some say that they have heard his ghost sneezing and coughing in the corridor outside the Vice President's office.

BISHOP SIMMS'S SONGS

Sometimes, when the hour is late, people have heard the distinctive, resonant voice of Bishop Simms drifting melodically from the Senate barbershop, where he was employed. Simms often worked late putting things in order for the next day. Often he would sing as he worked. James Ketchum, curator for the U.S. Senate, says that "Bishop" was a nickname, because Simms was "a man of the cloth on occasion." Ketchum adds that little is known of the Bishop's personal life, including what his church affiliation was. However, he says that the singing had a soothing effect on those who listened, and that Simms often would break into song during the day, too. It was a refreshing change from the talk of politics that usually dominated the Senate barbershop. However, there is one thing that has bothered some of those who have recently heard the Bishop in song —he has been dead a goodly number of years.

THE SLAIN LAWYER

Footsteps roaming the Capitol aren't the only late night sounds that have been experienced in the historic building. Moans and groans have been heard. Is it the wind that whips through cracks in the old mortar, or is it a cry from some of the departed souls who wrestled with this nation's problems in life, and have been unable to lay them down in death? It depends on whom you talk to. Some claim that moans heard from the basement beneath the old Supreme Court chamber in the Senate wing are cries of anguish from a young lawyer who died in a scuffle with a congressman. The two were supposedly arguing politics in what was the old record room of the court when the congressman, whose name has been lost, shoved the lawyer against the masonry wall. The lawyer's head split open. According to some Capitol Hill storytellers, his moans continue through the ages.

HENRY WILSON'S PERPETUAL TUBBING

Henry Wilson, Vice President in the Grant Administration, was among certain senators who frequently used the bathtubs in the lower Senate wing. The hand-carved marble tubs had been imported from Italy for the convenience of the senators. "Tubbing" was a popular pastime. Vice President Wilson, however, apparently caught a congestive chill on one of his tubbing ventures. It proved to be the death of him. That was in November of 1875, but the story only begins then.

It wasn't too many years later that people who were concerned with guarding the Senate side of the Capitol began to relate how they had seen a diaphanous Vice President Wilson returning from tubbing. They claim also to have heard the Vice President coughing and sneezing.

Legend has it that these stains on the stairs to the House press gallery are from the blood of Congressman William Taulbee, who was killed here by a reporter. His spirit still haunts the stairs.

Several times since the death of Henry Wilson, mysterious sneezes have been heard in the corridor leading to the Vice President's office. The unusual thing about it is that no one is ever there. There is just a damp chill in the doorway, and the faint scent of an old soap they used to provide for the senators' use in the basement tubs.

Should you be walking by the office of the Vice President on a Capitol tour and hear a sneeze, but see no one reacting, simply go on walking. The shade of Vice President Wilson may have just joined your tour.

BLOOD ON THE HOUSE GALLERY STAIRS

There has been violence in the Capitol, too. In the winter of 1890, former Congressman William Taulbee of Kentucky and newspaper reporter Charles Kincaid got into an argument on a stairway going up to the House gallery. A researcher for the U.S. Capitol Historical Society told me that the discussion apparently centered around some articles about Taulbee. The argument grew quite heated and ended when the former lawmaker was shot dead on the spot.

There are those who deny that the spots still visible on the stairs are stains from the congressman's blood, but some of the older guards and workers just smile. No cleaning agent has been able to remove those stains from the porous marble. Besides, some say they have heard—others swear they have seen—the spirit of the former congressman haunting that very spot. Every time a reporter stumbles on those old steps leading up to the Gallery, there are several Capitol employees who chuckle. You see, they think it may be Congressman Taulbee's spirit tripping the journalist just to show his distaste for the profession.

The shadowy apparition of Pierre Charles L'Enfant has been seen more than once pacing the corridors of the Capitol, where he still waits to be paid for his part in planning the Federal City.

BOISE PENROSE CATCHES UP

Republican boss Boise Penrose loved his Senate office. During the 1920's he often worked late at night, reading and researching his subject matter for the next day's debates. Penrose had no one close to him except his office staff, and he preferred the Capitol to his hotel home.

Some say that even now the Penrose spirit returns to the Senator's old office and sits in his favorite swivel chair during the late evening hours catching up on the *Congressional Record.*

THE CONTINENTAL SOLDIER PAYS HIS RESPECTS

The lower level of the Capitol, where George Washington was to have been entombed, is the haunting ground of at least two famous apparitions. The empty tomb, beneath the crypt area of the Capitol, is used to store the catafalque on which the nation's great lie in state. It is said that on certain days, at midnight and occasionally at noon, the locked door noiselessly swings open. Wind stirs the air and a cold spot envelops whoever might be watching, as a "fine-looking gentleman in Continental uniform" passes slowly around the bier, through the dark passage, and out the door, which silently closes behind him.

PIERRE L'ENFANT'S SORROWFUL VIGIL

Whenever modifications in the plan of Washington are being discussed within the walls of Congress, French engineer Pierre Charles L'Enfant—or I should say his spirit—is generally at the center of the discussion. A friend of the Marquis de Lafayette, he came over during the Revolution and conceived a grandiose plan for the Federal City in which he envisioned streets one hundred feet wide, and one avenue four hundred feet wide and a mile long. Many of those who looked over the Potomac pastureland and marshes, thought L'Enfant's plan was foolhardy. Nevertheless, President George Washington liked it, and with his endorsement the city began to take shape. There were delays, though, and L'Enfant was not as patient as the politicians. It wasn't long before his lack of tact and diplomacy got him into difficulties, including confrontations with Congress. He was taken off the job, and others completed his work. He died disillusioned with his adopted country, and so impoverished that he had to be buried in a pauper's grave on Digges Farm because Congress still hadn't paid him for his work.

It is said that some have encountered the shadowy figure of a small man, rather seedy in appearance, with a roll of parchment under his arm roaming the musty subterranean rooms of the Capitol. Often he is found pacing and shaking his head. Could it be that L'Enfant still walks the Capitol halls waiting for reparation, and determined to tell Congress how badly they treated him?

THE LIBRARIAN'S LOST CACHE

There was a time when the Library of Congress occupied a portion of the Capitol building. Its early years were marred by two fires, one in 1814 when the British burned Washington, and the second in 1851 when almost half the collection was destroyed. Yet the Library continued to grow and expand. In 1897 when its Capitol home became too small, it moved into an ornate Italian Renaissance structure across the street. However, one tale in particular is still told about the section of the Capitol that once housed the Congressional Library.

There was a librarian who became more prominently known after death than he was in life. In life he had been rather miserly, according to his associates. He had no friends, and some say he wasn't especially close to his family. His first love was money. Most of those who worked under him at the Library had heard that he did not trust Washington's banks, but no one knew where he hid his money.

As librarian, the old man had the advantage of knowing which books were not being used. He stashed his wealth in these forgotten volumes. One day he suffered a stroke, and died without ever being able to tell members of his family about his cache.

It wasn't until a few years later, when the Library was being moved across the street, that his hiding places were discovered. Workers are said to have found nearly six thousand dollars in various old volumes.

Stories still circulate around the Capitol that the spirit of the old librarian comes back to the area just to the west of the Rotunda where the Library was once located. They say his spirit searches for those long-removed shelves and the dusty books in which he hid his savings.

Long ago a miserly librarian stashed his savings in some of the dusty volumes that were on the shelves of the Library of Congress when it was in the Capitol. Even after the library moved to its own quarters across the street, his spirit continued to return to the library's former site to search for his lost money.

Some have sworn that they have heard invisible fingers frantically turning through invisible pages, as though the old man is condemned by his love for money to search in vain throughout eternity.

DEMON CAT

Perhaps the most infamous apparition in the Capitol isn't that of a man at all, but that of the dreaded Demon Cat. The cat is said to make its home in the catafalque storage area also.

During the last century, cats were kept at the Capitol as mousers. As the rat population decreased, the need for the cats also decreased. Some of them were taken home as household pets; many wandered off. Over the years the Capitol cat population dwindled to nothing, except for one highly unusual cat who stayed.

For just over one hundred years now, this phantom feline has roamed the darkened corridors of the U.S. Capitol—carefully choosing just when to appear and just whom to harass. The Demon Cat, as it is unaffectionately called, waits until the victim is alone and the hour is late. Some members of the nighttime protection service shudder at the thought of encountering "D.C." They have heard the tales and some have known the victims.

Just seeing a black cat walking toward them is enough to startle many, but an encounter with the Demon Cat is a truly traumatizing experience. One January not too long ago, a victim retold his encounter with D.C. As he walked down a chilly, darkened hallway, he saw a shadowy cat walking silently toward him. It looked as though the creature was swelling. The guard rubbed his eyes. It *was* swelling. The guard felt paralyzed as he stared into the glowing, piercing eyes that came closer and closer and grew larger and larger. The animal swelled to the size of a giant tiger, yet never lost its unmistakable catlike form. Its purring changed to a ferocious snarl. There was a deafening roar as the monstrous animal leaped—with claws extended—toward its victim. The guard couldn't move. His feet seemed nailed to the floor. He covered his face with his arms as the giant animal seemed just inches away from landing on him. He screamed.

Nothing happened. The Demon Cat vanished into thin air as the man screamed.

The trembling guard stood alone, the corridor deserted, the silence pierced only by his breathing. His limp body was covered in a cold, clammy sweat. He felt drained. The narrow marble hallway now reminded him of a tomb. The guard shuddered, tried to pull himself together, and headed back to his desk. For some reason he just didn't feel like finishing his rounds.

Down through the years there have been varied reactions from those who have encountered the phantom cat. Some have fainted. Some have run screaming from the building. Others—like the guard—became paralyzed with fear. Years ago, they tell me, old D.C.'s appearance just may have been what brought on one elderly guard's fatal heart attack.

The Demon Cat isn't one of the Capitol's most frequent visitors, but what it lacks in frequency it makes up for in accuracy as a portent. This most famous of all of the Capitol's legendary apparitions always appears just before a national tragedy or on the eve of the changing of an administration. Some cynical veterans of Capitol Hill argue that it is sometimes difficult to tell one of these events from the other, but make no mistake: congressmen, senators, staff workers, maintenance personnel, and protection staff all walk the Capitol halls in fear of encountering the dreaded Demon Cat, for they are convinced such a meeting is a warning of unpleasant events to come.

THE CURSE ON THE CAPITOL

For years there have been debates over the so-called infirmities of the Capitol. Some argue that the building is sinking on a less than firm foundation; others that the walls are crumbling. The Capitol has undergone many face-lifts since the day William Thornton designed it. The only part of the original building that can be seen from the outside is the West front. Quite visible, too, are the supports that hold it up.

There are those around Washington who sincerely believe there may be more to the Capitol infirmities than meets the eye. They recall how back in September

The catafalque storage area in the Capitol basement is said to be the home of the dreaded Demon Cat, which makes a chilling appearance just before a national tragedy or the changing of an administration.

The beams supporting the west front of the Capitol (above) and relieving the strain on some of its crumbling columns (below) are often pointed out by those who believe the Capitol is haunted by a curse from a dying workman.

of 1808, architect Benjamin Latrobe and his construction superintendent John Lenthall argued over the necessity of a particular arch for support. Lenthall contended that it was not only unnecessary but also unsightly. Latrobe felt otherwise. He told Lenthall that the support was designed to prevent stress and a possible collapse of the structure.

The headstrong Lenthall was determined to prove his point. In spite of La-

trobe's warning, he pulled out the support. John Lenthall was crushed to death by falling debris, and quite a few Washingtonians believe that his dying words were a curse on the U.S. Capitol.

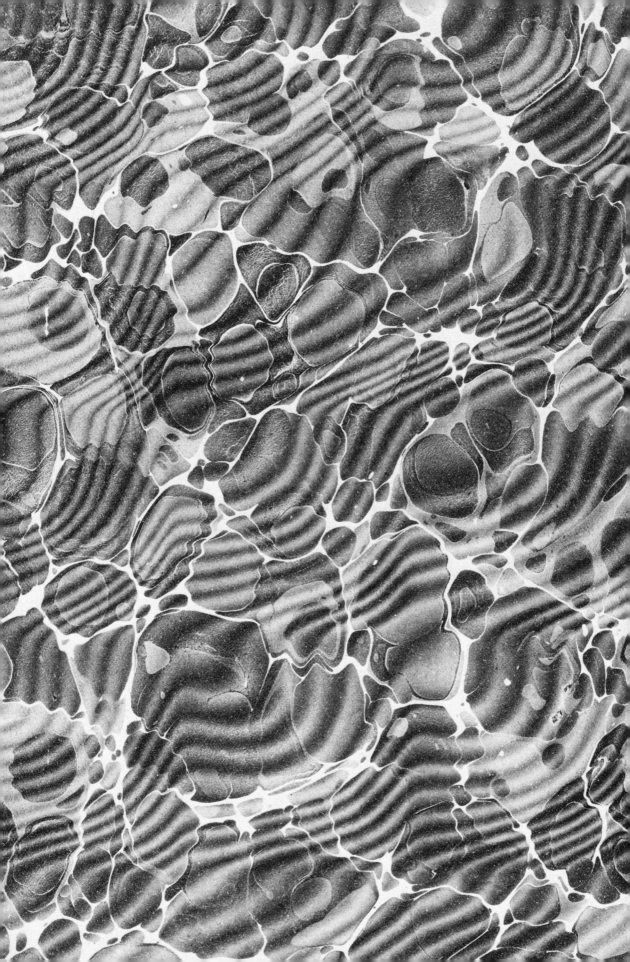

5. CAPITOL HILL

STRANGE HAPPENINGS AT THE OLD BRICK CAPITOL

If you are brave enough to venture out at night in the area of 1st and East Capitol Streets—directly behind the Capitol building—do not become alarmed if you encounter an airy figure or ethereal sounds that seem to enshroud the white marble of the United States Supreme Court building. You certainly won't be the first to do so. Some years ago a congressman who had risen just before dawn in order to get an early start on a mountain of paperwork that had piled up on his desk, had such a startling experience that he wasn't able to concentrate on anything else for quite some time.

The nation's highest court has not always occupied that corner. The Old Brick Capitol stood there and was torn down to make room for it earlier in this century. The Old Brick Capitol had survived many threats of demolition over the years, but as one elderly lady who had grown to love the building told me, "It was the determination of Chief Jus-

tice Taft that got it."

After the British had burned the Capitol during the War of 1812, Congress used the Old Brick Capitol as a temporary home for the five years it took to repair the Capitol. The people there on Jenkins Hill and elsewhere around town kept on calling the structure the Old Brick Capitol for several years afterward. Congress moved back into the new Capitol in 1819, and the Old Brick Capitol was divided into apartments and townhouses.

Among those who lived there was famed southern orator John C. Calhoun. The South Carolinian wore many political hats while serving his country. He was a congressman, a senator, a secretary of state, and a vice president.

Not too long before he died, Calhoun was visited in a vision by none other than George Washington. The spirit of the Father of the Country warned Calhoun of the growing movement toward secession. It is a matter of record that before his death in 1850, Calhoun correctly predicted the secession of the next decade. "The dissolution of the Union,"

warned Calhoun, "is the heaviest blow that can be struck at civilization and representative government."

Calhoun's spirit continued to roam through the Old Brick Capitol for years. Often-told tales recount how it was most restless when the federal government turned the building into a prison during the Civil War, as if concerned over the treatment of Confederate prisoners. It is a period not many like to remember.

One writer described the Old Brick Capitol complex as having been in a state of decay before the Union decided to take it over and turn it into a prison. It was "a dingy, crumbling structure, with rambling passages, and with quaint rooms where one least expected to find them." When the building was converted into a prison, iron bars were placed in the windows. "When occupied by prisoners," the caption to one old picture says, "its windows were generally crowded by its inmates, and passers-by were not al-

John C. Calhoun, who possessed psychic powers, rented an apartment in the Old Brick Capitol after Congress returned to its original quarters. His spirit is one of those said to have frequented the building in later years.

The Old Brick Capitol served as the temporary home of the Congress when the British burned the Capitol in 1814. It was later converted to residences and was used as a federal prison during the Civil War. Even though the site is now occupied by the Supreme Court building, it is still haunted by ghosts and apparitions of the Old Brick Capitol.

lowed to stop at any time on the opposite side of the street, lest they should attempt to communicate, by signs, with those within the prison." Long after the prisoners left the Old Brick Capitol the spirits of the captives and their jailers have continued to visit the site of their captivity.

The history of the building at 1st and East Capitol was the furthest thing from the mind of the unidentified congressman of the 1920's who had risen before dawn to get a head start on his paperwork. He was deep in thought about his constituents' problems as he walked along in the

chilly—and slightly foggy—morning. His first thought when he saw a man walking back and forth in front of the homes was that he wasn't the only person to brave the chill and venture out before sunup.

His train of thought interrupted by the pacing man ahead, the congressman began to notice something peculiar about the figure. The cadence of his movement seemed to be a march. There was something long protruding from over his shoulder. He wore a cap with an upturned bill and a saber sheathed at his waist.

The congressman blinked his eyes, scarcely believing what he saw. But he never had a chance to question the uniformed sentry, because at that moment the sun burned a hole through the fog and the guard instantly vanished—as though he was swallowed up by the sun's rays. The apparition had appeared near where the main entrance to the old prison had been.

The congressman just stood there. Finally, he managed to catch his breath, shake the image from his mind's eye, and move on to his office. It had so unnerved him, though, that he simply paced back and forth in his office, doing no work, and talking to no one. Never again would he doubt the whispers he had heard about the Old Brick Capitol.

Many of those whispers about the goings on inside and outside the old structure came from some of the members of the National Woman's Party. The building had been acquired by the suffragettes in 1922—long after remnants of the old prison had been ripped out. In addition to a headquarters for the movement, the old building—with its cells converted into bedrooms—served as a dormitory for the women. Although it had been over fifty years since anyone had been incarcerated within the building's walls, or executed in the courtyard, some of the tales told by the women would chill the hearts of the most skeptical.

The National Woman's Party workers were well aware of the building's past. They loved to boast of the distinguished Americans who had lived there and those who had been inside the house when it had served as a temporary capitol. More than one could guide guests to the rooms the Honorable Mr. Calhoun used when he lived there. The women also knew there were some not-so-glorious moments in the past, but they had learned to accept the fact that their home had also been a notorious federal prison.

Before her recent death, former resident, Mabel Vernon, a charter member of the National Woman's Party, was reminiscing about the old days of the women's movement. Although she was then retired, she had a clear recall not only of the political struggles, but also of some of the unusual events that had taken place in that house. She showed me yellowed clippings of newspaper stories concerning women who had worked there and heard

weird sounds and seen strange sights. Matter-of-factly she told me of "unexplainable incidents," as she called them, that she had heard about, but never witnessed herself.

Some of the National Woman's Party workers quoted in these articles from the late 1920's said that moaning, weeping, and sighing often kept them from sleeping. They never knew when peaceful slumber would be shattered by a maniacal scream or the reverberating clank of an invisible cell door slamming shut or the bitter laughter that drifted through the rooms.

Mabel Vernon told me, "We used to talk a lot about the old prison and some of the very notable spies who had been kept there." Some of the Lincoln assassination conspirators were among those incarcerated there. It has been suggested that it was the spirit of accused conspirator Mary Surratt who cried out in agony. On several anniversaries of Mary Surratt's death, the outline of a female figure was seen against one of the windows. One witness reported that the figure sobbed incessantly while clenching her "ghostly white fists against black iron bars" that were also a part of the apparition.

Some conjecture that the sounds of laughter heard in the building came from notorious Confederate spy Belle Boyd, returning to the place where she had spent many unhappy months. The attractive young woman had used her charms to gain confidence in many circles. She had "entertained" General Nathaniel Banks, for example, while Stonewall Jackson rode to victory in the Shenandoah Valley. Later Miss Boyd was caught and confined in the Old Brick Capitol.

Some of the women seemed to think the pacing sounds, which were frequently heard coming from one of the former cells, could have been the tormented spirit of Confederate prison camp commander Henry Wirtz. Thirteen thousand Federal soldiers had died while he was in charge of Andersonville. Wirtz spent the last days of his life in the Old Brick Capitol before he was led to the courtyard and hanged.

One incident, Mabel Vernon recalled,

Later occupants reported hearing bitter laughter, which they attributed to the spirit of Confederate spy Belle Boyd, who was imprisoned in the Old Brick Capitol.

involved the violin of a member. The seldom-used instrument was kept in the parlor. One evening some of the women in another part of the house heard music coming from that direction. Assuming that the musician had decided to spend a relaxing evening entertaining them, they made their way to the parlor. Imagine their surprise when they discovered no one there.

The violin was resting in its usual place, and the bow still hung on the wall. The women looked at each other silently as the mysteriously produced music continued. They searched the house, but found no violinist. A couple of the young women even checked outside to see if someone was playing a trick on them.

Later in the evening, after their nerves had calmed, Mabel Vernon said they discussed the incident. She recalled how a couple of the older women recognized the melody. They told her it was one of their favorites from the war. The Civil War. In their early childhood they had heard some of the old veterans humming it. It was the type of melody likely to have been a favorite in a prison where sad, lonely, and homesick soldiers wondered if they would ever be free to live and love again. The women never learned who their musically inclined visitor was, and even though that old melody drifted through the house on several other occasions, its origin was never discovered.

In spite of the supernatural visitors who walked its halls, the members of the National Woman's Party fought gallantly to save their beloved building—but the Supreme Court had outgrown its facilities, and Chief Justice William Howard Taft's determination to have the new quarters located on the land occupied by the Old Brick Capitol prevailed.

It has been nearly half a century since the white marble of the Supreme Court replaced the scarred old brick of the building that had been a temporary capitol, a temporary prison, a temporary rooming house, and a temporary headquarters for suffragettes. However, some say that if the time is right, and the moonbeams are glancing off the marble just a certain way, you may be able to see an apparition of the Old Brick Capitol shimmering before the building that dared to replace it. Some say the air even develops a stale, musty odor, and sometimes sobs, cries, and the distant clank of a cell door can be heard—if you hang around long enough.

THE GASLIGHT SPECTER

A 1935 *Washington Post* article by Gaeta Wold Boyer told about how she was investigating stories of supernatural occurrences at the First Spiritualist Church on C Street and was told by its minister how he had received his inspiration to become a minister from an encounter in his childhood with the phantom of a young woman.

As a young boy, at the turn of the century, the minister had lived with his family in a house on G Street. The minister recalled how his family happened on the spirit quite by accident. One chilly evening they were enjoying quiet fellowship on their porch when the father, deciding they would need a fire for warmth later that night, went to prepare it. Inside the doorway he struck a match to ignite the gaslight. The flame flickered, sputtered, and then caught, suffusing the room with a soft glow. Just about then the father cried out. The minister said that he and his brothers and sisters rushed in to see their father virtually paralyzed. His eyes were glued to a nearby couch. There stretched out on the sofa with "her hair over the arm rest" was a beautiful, but obviously lifeless young girl.

The reporter quotes the minister as saying that his father began to regain his composure, examine his feelings, and experiment. The father turned the light to a fuller flame, and the figure vanished. He dimmed the light and the specter reappeared. He repeated the procedure twice more, with the same results. With the presence of the spirit also came the strong odor of gas. As the fumes permeated the room, the girl's complexion and clothing became radiant; she shimmered in the soft light. When coughing broke the silence, she vanished. Then, startled out of his trancelike state, the father became concerned about his family's safety and ushered everyone back outside while he searched for the source of the gas fumes.

The minister said that they were too shaken to discuss the encounter, so they just sat staring into the darkness until their father pronounced the house free of gas. No one slept that night, and most of the family were out of their bedrooms by first light, going over what had happened and trying to understand what it meant. By midmorning it had been decided that they would question the neighbors, check the real estate records, and do what else was necessary to help them learn who the young lady haunting their house had been, and whether others had had encounters similar to theirs.

The family learned the identity of the ghost from a neighbor. The young woman had lived in the house several decades earlier. She had become so disillusioned with life, and so despondent after her fiancé was killed in the Civil War, that a permanent sleep seemed her only answer. Legend has it that she slowly dressed for bed, turned up the gas, and then lay down on the sofa in the parlor to dream her last dream of the handsome young man in the blue uniform who would have been hers had not a cannonball at Manassas separated them. It is said that a smile came to her lips at the thought of rejoining him, and that she entered her deepest sleep.

This encounter was the beginning of the minister's lifelong interest in the supernatural. He told the *Post* reporter his tale in his church office. She reported that it was not unusual for those who chatted with him there to be interrupted by a door opening or a chair scraping across the floor of its own volition, or to see a book move across the minister's desk without help from human hands. The old church is no longer there. It was torn down to make way for a newer structure. The minister is long gone, too —free to join his friends on the other side.

A MURDERED MAN'S REVENGE

For many years before the turn of the century there was a dilapidated house in Southwest Washington that was haunted by the spirits of a young woman and a young man who are believed to have lost their lives there. In sharp contrast to the well-cared-for homes in the area and the manicured lawn of the Capitol just opposite, "the house with the ghostly stare," as it has been referred to, was in need of repair, and its yard was overgrown with vines and weeds.

A rusted iron fence separated the dismal yellow-brick structure from the sidewalk, yet passers-by preferred the other side of the street. I have heard that the old house was once owned by a rich young man who, storytellers say, never wanted for female companionship. He is supposed to have dined with a young lady late one evening by candlelight, and perhaps had a little too much to drink. After a delectable dinner, the charming host lured his companion down into the cellar, where he had stored a remarkable collection of foreign wines—almost all of which he had brought into the country himself from his travels abroad. The young woman resisted his advances and they quarreled.

How the young man died in that cool, dank, and dimly lighted cellar remains a mystery. None of the articles I read nor any of the people with whom I talked could shed much light on it, although one old-timer had heard that the young woman had defended her honor with a wine bottle, which she broke over the young man's head. According to some accounts, she left the house screaming and found a policeman. The police questioned her and let her go. According to another version, she slipped out of the house unnoticed. In both stories she returned the next morning to see whether her victim was dead, and never came out again.

Stories sprang up on Capitol Hill that the house was cursed by the young man's spirit, which is filled with "intense hatred" for those of the "same sex and age of his slayer." Within a few years some residents began to tell of the shadowy form of a young woman in mourning who would unlatch the wrought iron gate, climb the steps, and enter the house.

One writer around the turn of the century stated, "Few persons have remained long in the house, although it has been variously occupied." That reporter admitted to having masqueraded as a spiritualist in order to find out about one woman's experience in the house. However, he confessed in the article, "with remarkable quickness . . . the lady divined" his profession, and told him of her experiences anyway. She said that her family lived in the old house for a brief time during the 1880's when she was in her late teens. Her father had known the gossip about the house, but shrugged it off when he bought it.

Shortly after they moved in, her father was standing "in the house when a woman dressed in deep mourning passed through the hall and up the stairs." Her father pursued the shadow, but found nothing on either the second or third floors. Later, a maid encountered the same shadow, and afterward refused to return to the house.

The *Washington Times* recorded the young woman's eyewitness story of her encounter with what she believed was the violent spirit of the vengeful young man. She said the frightening episode occurred on an evening when her mother and father were not at home. Since the spirit had not made its presence known before, I assume that, as is true in most ghost stories, the appearance was on the anniversary of his death. She told the reporter who interviewed her that she suddenly became frozen with fear, and a numbness permeated her body. Her vocal chords were paralyzed so that she could not cry out.

She recalled, "I felt myself losing shape!" but as she regained the power of motion, she began running around the room in a desperate battle for possession of her own spirit. The strong-willed young woman's youthful body succeeded in holding onto her spirit, but the concentration it took to ward off such a cunning and violent attack drained her and she lapsed into unconsciousness.

Workmen coming to repair the house the next morning found her lying in her own blood. She told the reporter that the blood came from a wound "right across the bridge of my nose." The article says that the wound healed in the shape of the figure 7.

After that family moved, there were a few other brave souls who gave the house a try. Even the Red Cross made a stab at using it as an office, but moved within a few weeks. Tales of encounters persisted for more than a quarter of a century, making the house so undesirable that no one would live there. After having been unoccupied for several years, it was finally torn down. In the years since, with the house gone, the old stories have all but vanished, too.

HONEYMOON HOUSE

In the 1840's a handsome home was built on Capitol Hill as a wedding gift to a young couple. Some articles referred to it as the Honeymoon House. The couple was joyously looking forward to sharing their love and their lives in that home, but when night descended on their wedding day it brought a terrible cloud that was never lifted from the house. That very night the groom mysteriously vanished.

An article in the *Washington Star* said the young man "was reputed to be wealthy," but no one ever found his riches. They searched his bank box, but it contained only some worthless C & O Canal stock. Some believed that the man had simply deserted his wife, but rumors that he had gone to his farm in Virginia were denied by his relatives, who also expressed concern about him. Several years went by, according to the *Star* article, and then someone found a body on his farm. Word spread rapidly that it was the body of the missing bridegroom, but a doctor who examined it said it wasn't. The skeleton was a good foot taller. "The mystery lingered," said the *Star*.

The bride could shed no light on her husband's whereabouts. She could offer no reason for his disappearance, only tears and uncontrollable sobs. She was, a

Washington Post article had earlier reported, "a tall, handsome brunette with flashing dark eyes . . . possessed of an extraordinary mind; she was equally capable of holding her own through scholarly argument or by quick, biting repartee or veiled sarcasm." But after her husband vanished, she never really recovered, and the mere mention of her lover's name would send her into a trancelike daze, or trigger more sobbing. She refused to believe he would not return, and for that reason, never left the house.

The bride remained inside her honeymoon house alone. Reportedly, she spent her days polishing silver and cleaning and caring for the many wedding gifts. Some say she spent her evenings preparing for the wedding night that had been interrupted. The house fell into decay, and eventually the health authorities condemned it. When a neighbor urged her to move to more comfortable surroundings, a *Post* article written in 1903 a few years after her death says, "The solitary old soul glanced silently but lovingly at the dingy walls, the threadbare furniture, the big lumbering piano with its dull mahogany boards and yellow ivory keys . . . and shaking her head sadly but resolutely, she replied 'This is good enough for me.' "

The old lady told the solicitous neighbor, "So long as you see the shades on my front window up you will know all's well." Within a few days the neighbor noticed that the shades were drawn. He tried to enter, but the door was barred from the inside. Inside he heard moans and groans. Rushing to the corner, he hailed a policeman. It was, however, too late. The woman lay dying on her parlor floor, blood streaming from under her head. She had evidently been stricken with "paralysis" and had fallen and hit her head while trying to reach the sofa. There were cuts and gashes on her cheek and brow. The woman had lived alone in that huge house for more than half a century. Is it any wonder that tales of her spirit's returning to the old house made the newspapers? Until the house was torn down in the 1930's, there were accounts of "a little old lady with a kerosene lamp" who walked through the hallways. One source who was brave enough to enter, described the air as "scented and cold." No one wanted the old house. Its decay was a blight on Capitol Hill, so it was removed. Where does the restless spirit of the bride search for her wandering husband now?

The ghost of Joseph Holt, who sentenced Mary Surratt, has been reported wandering Capitol Hill in search of more evidence of her guilt or innocence.

THE REMORSE OF THE HEARTLESS JUDGE

The Lincoln assassination conspiracy and its aftermath reached out to touch still another life. Judge Advocate General Joseph Holt, who had been the presiding judge at the conspiracy trial and had insisted on the death penalty for Mary Surratt, was said to have changed dramatically afterward. Holt, who was from Kentucky, had apparently never been well liked in Washington. Once, when he was commissioner of patents, his boss recommended him for promotion to Postmaster General of the United States because "he has no heart." Gerald Cullinan, in his book *The Post Office Department,* says, "he was taciturn, vindictive, and ill-mannered." Attitudes toward Holt didn't change after the conspirators were hanged, and he began increasingly to lead the life of a recluse. Newspaper articles from that period say he withdrew into the privacy of his home, which was described as decaying, with bars on the windows, and shades that never permitted the sun's rays inside.

One reporter in the late 1880's said that the once-manicured garden of Holt's house had become an "overgrowth of weeds and tangled vines." Children crossed the street to avoid the old house, which stood only a few blocks from the Old Brick Capitol Prison where Mary Surratt was originally incarcerated. Judge Holt apparently spent the remainder of his years in almost total solitude. Infrequently, he would venture out to buy food, but he is said to have much preferred to be sequestered in his shadowy surroundings, among his many volumes. Neighbors were quoted by one writer as saying, "His irrevocable decision weighed heavily upon him," and they speculated that he spent his time re-reading the transcripts of the famous trial.

After Holt's death, the new owners of his house worked diligently to make it a cheerful, warm home, but the presence of the departed "man with no heart" is said to have chilled more than one room. The sound of someone pacing in the upstairs library is reported to have often lasted for hours. Capitol Hill residents were sure they knew who it was. They used to tell of a remorseful Judge Advocate General Joseph Holt, sentenced to an eternity of pacing back and forth while reading over and over again the testimony taken at the trial of the Lincoln conspirators.

When the old house was torn down, the story changed somewhat. The Judge has been seen when the hour is late, clad in his midnight blue Union uniform, with cape pulled tightly about him, walking

down 1st Street. According to the legend, he is headed to the Old Brick Capitol to try to learn the truth from Mary Surratt.

*Those convicted in the assassination plot
against President Lincoln met their deaths on
the scaffold. Some say that Judge Advocate
General Joseph Holt was never able to erase
from his mind the memory of the hanging
of Mary Surratt and the other conspirators.*

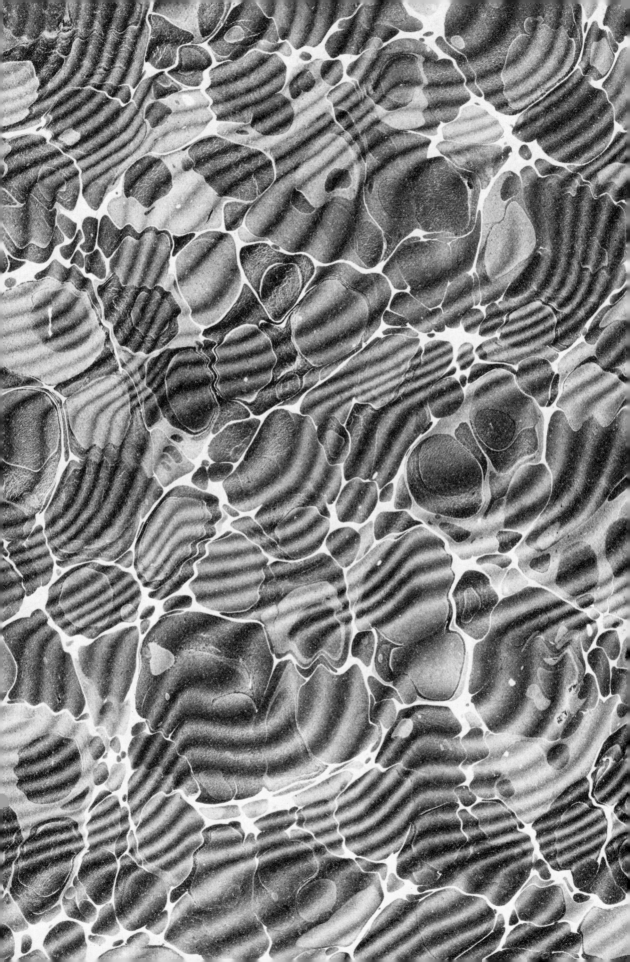

6. MILITARY TALES

The building on the right is the Marine Commandant's home, which is revisited periodically by the spirit of the Corps's first Commander.

THE RETURN OF THE MARINE COMMANDANT

The military quarters of the Federal City are not without their apparitions and ghosts. The Marines, for instance, have some tales that have been passed on through the years. The old Marine Corps Barracks and Parade Grounds have been standing for nearly two hundred years on 8th Street, between G and I Streets, in Southeast Washington. The Marine Corps commandant's home is exactly what one would expect the quarters of a high military official to look like. The furnishings are sparse and functional, relieved only by mementos of the Corps's long history and by portraits of former commandants. It seems strange that unexplainable events could take place in so regimented a setting. But they do, and some have even occasioned newspaper stories. Sounds of "rustling papers" fill the house in the darkness of night. Sometimes "the measured pacing of a man, deep in thought" is heard. The shade of a former commandant in the full dress uniform of the Corps's early years has been seen in various rooms.

One reporter earlier in this century speculated that it is the spirit of the Corps's first commandant, Captain Samuel Nicholas, though no one has ever been able to get close enough to distinguish the features of the shade. Legend has it that Captain Nicholas periodically returns to survey the home, and perhaps to learn what new glories have been celebrated by the fighting body he once led.

OLD HOWARD

There is a less famous old leatherneck who is said to revisit the frame house in which he once lived at the rear of the Marine garrison. "Old Howard," as he was referred to in newspaper accounts, lived about 100 years ago, in a two-story home with his wife and family near 9th and G Streets, Southeast.

Being a Marine was all Howard knew. He joined the Corps as a youth and adopted it as his parents. He spent his time trying to measure up to its tradition as he saw it. However, Howard's life in the service wasn't easy. Howard had a reputation for being a fighter. Breaking rules and regulations had lost him his sergeant's stripes more than once. His life at home wasn't easy either. He didn't get along with his wife and children any better than he got along with his fellow Marines. A *Washington Star* reporter said in 1871 that he "finally died blaspheming his Maker, and cursing his wife and children."

Legend has it that when "fearfully wicked" Howard died, his spirit dedicated itself to trying to uphold the man's mortal reputation. Over the years—and it has been well over a century since Howard died—there have been several tales about the pranks of a poltergeist

This account from the October 14, 1871, Washington Star *is the first official report that old Howard had not been slowed down by death.*

WASHINGTON'S HAUNTED HOUSE.
The Ghost of a Wicked Marine.

HE MAKES THINGS LIVELY IN HIS OLD HOME.

The neighborhood of 9th street, between G and H streets southeast, has been the scene of great excitement this week, in consequence of stories in circulation that a two-story frame house in the rear of the garrison, occupied by a family named Bonehart, is haunted by the ghost of its former occupant, a marine by the name of Howard. He was the owner of the house, and died there some eight or nine months since. He is represented to have been

A FEARFULLY WICKED MAN,

who abused his family and all around him, and finally died blaspheming his Maker and cursing his wife and children. His widow and children soon moved from the premises, not being able to sleep on account of hearing strange noises in the house, and they rented it to the Bonehart's, who took possession about two months since, not hearing anything about the house being haunted. This family, soon after moving in, became very uncomfortable; they could not sleep at night, and all became very nervous. They allege that

STRANGE NOISES

were heard every night, which they could not account for. Doors would be found open which had been previously locked. When the family were on the lower floor loud rappings would be heard up stairs, and when the family were in the upper rooms the rappings would appear to be below, as if some one was striking a table with a rattan stick. The back door would be found open after it had been carefully bolted, and when it was closed loud knocks were sometimes heard on the outside, making it shake. This was at first thought to be done by some one on the outside, but during its continuance the family would look out from an upper window immediately above, and nothing could be seen, although the knocking would continue. A blind door connecting with the next house, and which had been securely fastened up for years, was on several occasions found wide open, and no one could account for that. On Tuesday night last, a colored girl living with the Boneharts retired to bed in an upper room at rather a late hour, and when almost asleep she suddenly heard steps softly ascending the stairs, and saw the reflection of what was apparently a lighted lamp, but believing it was some member of the family, she did not trouble her mind about it, until hearing a heavy groan by the door, which stood ajar, she raised up in bed, and says she saw

THE GHOST OF OLD HOWARD.

The light in his lamp was at once extinguished, and blue and red streaks of light shot through the room. At one bound she was up and raising a frightful scream, which roused the whole house, she bolted down stairs and left the house in her night clothes, the entire family following her. The colored girl could not be induced to return to the house, but Bonehart and his family did, and after they had retired they heard terrible groaning from up stairs. Bonehart persuaded his wife that it was the window shutters swinging in the wind, although he did not believe it himself.

THE GHOST UNDER A BED.

Very soon the bed in which they were laying began to move out into the middle of the room, and loud groans came from underneath it. This so frightened them that they left the house, and Bonehart went to the station-house, where he told his story. Officer O'Hare at once repaired to the place, and found the family running away from the house. He examined the premises throughout, but could find nothing wrong, and persuaded them to return, promising that he would watch in the house. After they had retired he heard the noises and rapping and thought some one was at the back door, as the knob moved very perceptibly. He kept the family quiet, however, until morning and left them. The next night these scenes were enacted over again, and on being notified O'Hare and his partner, Shelton, stayed there again until about 12 o'clock, when nothing further being heard, the officers advised the family to go to bed, which they did, and the officers then left. After they left,

THE MOST UNEARTHLY NOISES

were again heard, much worse than ever, and the family became so much frightened that they left the premises and took shelter in the house of Mr. De Neal, a neighbor. Yesterday morning Bonehart was seeking another house in which to move, declaring that he would not stop there another night.

The neighborhood is greatly excited over the strange manifestations. We have told the story just as it is related by the Boneharts, their neighbors, and the policemen, and every reader can furnish his own explanation.

that sounds like Howard chronicled in newspaper accounts.

From the outset Howard's spirit showed no one mercy. His wife and children couldn't stand to remain in the house after he died. They sold it, probably quite cheaply. Life was more miserable with him gone; when he was alive they could at least see him when he was around.

Howard's spirit seemed to love the element of surprise. He would rap loudly when a person least expected it. That was only for openers. The old cuss would shake doors in the middle of the night just so he could watch groggy people stumble across the blackness from the bed to the door, and laugh at their expression when they discovered no one was there. It was enough to rattle anyone's brain.

A few days after one unnamed family moved into the house, Howard apparently caught sight of the couple's daughter. Even the apparel most young women of the early 1900's wore to bed couldn't hide her shapely body. Never having been accused by any of his brawling buddies of being a prude, Howard sprang into action. As the young lady turned off the gaslight and pulled up the covers, he pulled the covers back and began to pant and sigh. The daughter was so frightened she must have screamed several times before her shaking hand could relight the gas. Shivering and sobbing with terror, she cautiously surveyed every shadow in her shimmering room. Her hands tightly clutched the retrieved covers at her neck. The writer said that the family moved within a few days.

Howard's bawdy ghost seemed unable to resist bedroom pranks. He allegedly pulled a bed with a man and his wife on it out into the center of their bedroom. Shock wasn't enough; Howard wanted embarrassment too, so he flung open the shutters on the bedroom window.

According to the legend, the poor couple was so upset it was easier for them to move than to face their neighbor, who had been sitting on his porch that evening. In recent times, Howard's exploits haven't received as much notice. Perhaps they have become less frequent, or stopped altogether. Maybe there is sex after death. I can think of no other distraction that would have diverted the pesky poltergeist from his pranks.

THE FAITHFUL NAVY COMMANDANT

Call it interservice rivalry if you will, but the Navy's original commandant occasionally surveys his old home grounds too. Captain Thomas Tingey supervised the building of the Washington Navy Yard from his home—Quarters A—during the second decade of the nineteenth century. It was also Captain Tingey who personally set fire to the yard in 1814 to keep it from falling into the hands of the advancing British troops; and it was the same Captain Tingey who directed the Navy Yard's reconstruction after that war.

For some twenty-four years, Captain Thomas Tingey lived in the rambling mansion that had been built by Benjamin Latrobe. He and his wife had become quite reluctant to part from it—even in death. Old newspaper articles say that Captain Tingey willed the home to his wife, but the government had other ideas. The Navy fought and won the right to retain possession of the property.

Apparently that bitter battle in the courts didn't sit too well with the spirit of Captain Thomas Tingey. The ghost of the harassed commandant has been seen regularly down through the years—looking out from the upper windows of the mansion—surveying the Navy Yard he helped to build, and defying the Navy to evict him. Some say he holds no malice for his successors, and a few of his successors swear he provided them with inspiration. Captain Thomas Tingey just doesn't seem to want to leave his post.

The house next to the flagpole (above) is Quarters A, built for Navy Commandant Thomas Tingey. His ghost still frequents the place, keeping an eye on the house and activities at the Navy Yard. Left, a more recent photograph of the Tingey house.

THE MURDEROUS HOST

Although Washington itself was spared the battles of the Civil War, there was much fighting in the suburbs. It was there during this period that a bizarre tale of the supernatural had its origin.

Three unsuspecting soldiers were given sanctuary from the enemy and shelter from the elements in an old house just across the District line in Maryland. They had become separated from their group during a skirmish and decided not to try to find it again until morning.

Morning never came for the three soldiers.

Their host was of a different political persuasion. The welcome they had received was simply a trap. He bludgeoned all three to death as they slept soundly on the floor by the fire.

The host had an easy enough time disposing of the bodies and was never tried for the murder. The three soldiers were written off as battle casualties. But, legend says, their host had a difficult time removing the crimson stain on the floor of the bedroom where the three soldiers had died. No matter how hard he scrubbed, the bloodstains remained. Consequently, he kept a rug over the spot. After all, too many questions could be dangerous.

Whether the man died or moved away isn't known, but there were a series of owners down through the next few decades. Although none of them knew for certain just what the dark stains on the bedroom floor were, there is no denying that the strange things that occurred in that room may have led them to suspect the worst—particularly when it was discovered that even paint would not permanently cover the stains, if we accept one reporter's account of attempts to expunge them.

Another peculiarity of the room was that the large oak door to the hallway would never stay closed. As soon as you bolted it and turned away, the creaking of the bolt-action lock and the squeaking of the hinge sent the terrifying message. It wasn't necessary to turn around to know that the door was open again.

According to the story, the three soldiers have continued to keep watch in that room. Perhaps they are trying to atone for their careless mistake of not alternating as lookouts, of not bolting the large oak door, of trusting, in time of war, someone they did not know.

Some think a supernatural occurrence in that house caused the death of one owner. A yellowed newspaper report from the 1920's said that the man was seated in the bedroom where all the mysterious occurrences originated when suddenly the French doors onto the balcony were ripped from their hinges and flung to the ground. They did not break. Neighbors were quoted as saying that the man went into a state of shock from which he never recovered. What else he may have seen or heard was never revealed, for within a few days he died.

One version of this story has it that curious neighbors got to checking the background of the house after hearing the legend. They are supposed to have learned that their recently departed neighbor had the misfortune to have the same last name as the murderous host who had lived in the home during the Civil War.

Finding people willing to live in the

old house became more difficult. It fell into a state of disrepair, and not too many years ago those owning the property decided the house must be torn down. It was—as so many local houses haunted by spirits have been over the years.

THE GHOSTS OF THE PENSION BUILDING

"Meigs Old Red Barn" is what some Washingtonians called the Pension Building (today we call it the National Building Museum) after it was constructed in the 1880's. Some claim that the specter of General Montgomery Meigs is one of those that often materializes and frightens workers who are in the building at night.

America's war veterans, their widows, and their children, have not collected pensions inside "Meigs Old Red Barn" —as the Pension Building between F and G and 4th and 5th Streets, Northwest, used to be called—in over fifty years. It has been even longer since the last presidential inaugural ball was staged there, yet tales of supernatural events and spectral encounters have led to speculation that more than one old-timer may still frequent the huge hall. In fact, in recent years at least one person has been committed to a mental institution because he believed he had met up with one of them inside the old Pension Building.

The building, which one newspaper of the late 1880's described as "the largest brick building in the world," is located to the north of Judiciary Square. It is presently being used by the District of Columbia courts, but it is slated for eventual use by the Smithsonian Institution as a museum.

Unchanged on the outside since it was built in 1885, the Pension Building stands on the bloodstained ground where the first wounded and dying from the Battle of Bull Run were brought. At one time this was also the site of the District jail and an asylum for the insane.

The Pension Building was conceived by U.S. Quartermaster General Montgomery C. Meigs. One newspaper reporter said that he fancied himself an architect, but many Washingtonians considered him simply an eccentric. Another newspaper account compared his design of the Pension Building with the famous Farnese Palace in Rome, and said it was his strong will rather than good sense that prevailed when the final plans for the building were approved.

One of the few areas in which the General had to compromise was in material for the huge interior Corinthian columns. He wanted to import solid onyx, but the government wouldn't foot the bill. The General had to settle for simulated onyx, but only after a worldwide search for a craftsman uncovered a Canadian so talented that few professionals could tell his onyx wasn't the real thing.

Another feature of these monumental columns is their hollow interiors, which Meigs is supposed to have used as an archive. He is reported to have collected secret government documents, letters of state, artifacts of all sorts, along with other mementos of the period, and personally salted them away in one or more of the columns. No one really knows what might be concealed in any of them, or in the various nooks and crannies of the building.

Soon after the mammoth structure was completed, President Grover Cleveland staged his inaugural ball there. Washington papers were filled with stories—among them several about the guest list, which included such notables as General William T. Sherman, Buffalo Bill Cody, and Frederick Douglass. One local newspaper article boasted that the Pension Building was "looked upon as one of the attractions of Washington." But critics called it an "unsightly monstrosity" and loved to repeat the remark made by General Philip Sheridan during a tour of the building. When the guide proudly stated that the fifteen-million-brick structure was fireproof, Sheridan exclaimed, "What a pity."

It was in 1917 that strange happenings were first reported in the Pension Building. One night an old guard sat at his desk and stared in disbelief at one of the huge columns as the simulated onyx began to change its configuration. By the light of his gas lamp, the guard saw the veins slowly shift to form the outline of an Indian, and farther down—a buffalo head! Although he was considerably unnerved, the old man talked himself out of running away. He convinced himself that he had dreamed the whole thing.

By the light of the morning sun, he carefully examined the column. The strange profiles that had been created before his eyes were still there. It was about then that his relief showed up with the morning paper. There on the first page was a story about the death of Buffalo Bill Cody—who had been the center of attention at the first presidential inaugural ball staged in the great hall of the Pension Building. He had died the previous evening.

The forms of an Indian and of a buffalo head appeared on columns of the Pension Building (now the National Building Museum) when Buffalo Bill died. He was one of the notables who attended the first Presidential inaugural ball staged there.

A few months later someone noticed the outline of a skull. Several smaller skulls were also discovered in the marble, but none was like the one referred to in newspaper accounts as the "malevolent, grinning skull." It appeared a short time after the buffalo head incident, and some old guards said it seemed to follow them wherever they went in the great hall.

As the years went by and more and more people visited the great hall, whispers began to develop about other strange swirls that had appeared in the columns. A newspaper article in the 1920's said that there were those who insisted that the formations resembled the profiles of George and Martha Washington, but that anyone reporting such configurations was scoffed at. However, the frequency with which new—and changing—patterns were being noticed in the columns of the Pension Building continued to attract attention. Newspapers devoted pages—complete with photographs —to the unfolding drama.

These changing patterns in the columns, along with some startling encounters with shadowy forms, made for short tenure among those who were assigned to watch the building at night. When the District altered the building for use by the courts, the planners—perhaps encouraged by acute personnel problems—covered over the simulated onyx that General Meigs loved so much. But even though the anomalous profiles are a thing of the past, the renovation has had little effect on the spirits that come calling from time to time.

It wasn't too long ago that a night watchman took a prescribed leave of absence to recuperate from an encounter with an ill-tempered man on horseback. Old-timers say that there was a period when one of the upper floors was used to quarter horses. It was there that the guard encountered a rider in military uniform who spurred his transparent mount down the corridor toward the wide stairway. The horse almost rode down the night watchman, who fled the building in panic.

I first learned of the watchman's experience from an attorney who practices law in the District of Columbia Superior Court, now quartered in the old Pension Building. He said he had discussed it with the chief judge and several other lawyers—all of whom expressed concern. Some of the men who were involved in renovating the building at the time were also anxious. They had heard stories about the changing column patterns and about other visits by a horseman. A few who had known the watchman, openly admitted that they would never again enter the place at night—job or no job.

Some believe that General Meigs's spirit is the ill-tempered rider on horseback who comes to the old building— particularly during periods of renovation. They seem to think that a man of such strong will would certainly possess a spirit capable of watching over his cathedral to insure its preservation.

The transparent rider on horseback has not been the only spirit encountered in the old Pension Building. Late one summer night in 1972 one of the security personnel was reading a newspaper behind the information desk on the ground level when he noticed a man in a light-colored suit with a peculiar walk moving quietly toward the stairway. Some of his fellow workers told a lawyer that the guard followed the strange-looking man to the third floor. Just as he got close enough to ask the man how he had penetrated the locked doors, and what his business was, the man turned. The watchman opened his mouth to speak, but out came a nightmarish yell. He covered his face and then ran wildly from the building.

Sometime later that night, I was told, a patrolling police car noticed a man who appeared to be in a daze walking down the middle of Pennsylvania Avenue. Checking his identification, the officers learned where the man worked. Within an hour or so, the watchman's supervisor and a doctor were talking with him. Much of what he said, however, was incoherent. He remained in a state of shock and often broke into uncontrollable sobs. About all the doctor could get out of the watchman was that he had looked at a man with no eyes in his head, and had seen the fires of hell and smelled the stench of the dead.

One of the lawyers, who closely fol-

The simulated marble columns inside the Pension Building, which is now the National Building Museum, were painted over after guards and visitors told tales of changing configurations in the veins. But in spite of renovations like this, tales of supernatural happenings haven't stopped.

lowed the security officer's experience, told me that the man was committed to Saint Elizabeth's Hospital for extensive psychiatric treatment.

No one has yet explained how the man with a peculiar walk, wearing a light-colored suit, was able to enter the tightly locked building—or how he managed to leave it.

a shorthand clerk, and he was the Bureau of Ordinance stenographer pressed into service by Secretary of War Edwin Stanton the night President Lincoln was shot. It was Tanner who transcribed the testimony from witnesses at Ford's Theatre. In later years, he turned that tragedy into a livelihood. Billed as "Corporal Tanner," he became a celebrated lecturer and public speaker. The job as pension commissioner came in 1889 but lasted only briefly. Tanner was dumped by the administration because he increased veterans' pension payments without approval.

However, those who believe that Tanner is the man in the light-colored suit don't believe his visits have anything to do with pensions; they think they are connected with his role as an authority on the Lincoln assassination. They recall how Lincoln's son Robert, as Secretary of War in the 1880's, approved the plans for the Pension Building. Robert Lincoln was inclined to think that there was more to the Lincoln death conspiracy than the public was ever told, and some believe that he may have been persuaded by Meigs to hide important documents and secret material connected with his father's death in one of those Corinthian columns. Perhaps he was convinced that if the real truth were known it would shake the public's faith in their form of government. After all, they point out, the country was only a little over one hundred years old at the time and in the midst of trying to pull itself together after a bloody and divisive Civil War.

Many who knew Quartermaster General Montgomery Meigs say he had visions of those Corinthian columns standing for centuries—much as the columns of ancient Greece have survived the destruction of most tangible evidence of that civilization. It seems logical, the reasoning goes, that Robert might have given such important material to the ages rather than destroy it.

Some think that Tanner felt he knew the full story but never had the proof, and that he is sometimes drawn back to the building in his eternal search for evidence.

Some students of the old Pension Building think the man in the light-colored suit could have been the spirit of one of the first pension commissioners, James Tanner, a famed champion of Civil War veterans. Corporal Tanner had lost both feet in the Second Battle of Bull Run, which would explain the odd gait. After Bull Run, Tanner was retrained as

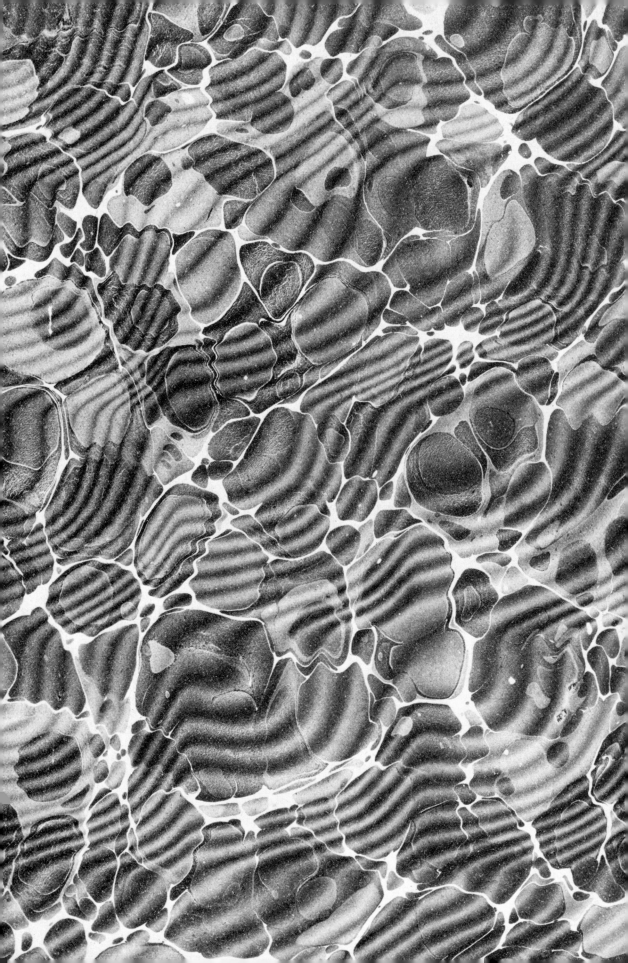

7. OTHER TALES

GEORGE WASHINGTON RIDES AGAIN

George Washington's plantation stretched south and east, from near the Federal District almost to Williamsburg, Virginia. Often he would make social calls on the Byrds of Westover, the Lees of Stratford, and the Carters of Shirley. He would ride up to Alexandria for fellowship too. Whether the General saw any of the ghosts that are said to frequent those old Virginia mansions is strictly conjecture, but there is some evidence that Washington, at least once, had an encounter with something that shook him tremendously.

It supposedly happened as he was working on a dispatch, alone in his tent, during the Revolutionary War. *The National Tribune* reported in a story in 1880 that Washington aide Anthony Sherman said that the General had confided in him that "a beautiful female figure" spread America's future before him. The spirit unfolded a vision that included not only Washington's successes, but the nation's international destiny, too.

Some have theorized that the thought of that vision was with the President when he wrote his farewell address. In that speech he warned against permanent alliance with foreign powers, big public debt, a large military establishment, and the devices of "small, artful, enterprising minorities" to control or change the government.

Washington retired to Mount Vernon to live out the remainder of his years. Some who have worked there swear that he comes back from time to time. There have been various accounts down through the years of the General riding on horseback across his estate to the stables, much in the way he did on his last ride, on a cold and rainy December night so long ago.

Some say that on certain moonlit nights the ghost of George Washington can be seen riding his favorite horse across his estate toward Mount Vernon, just as he did on his last ride before he died.

THE INFAMOUS BLADENSBURG DUELING GROUNDS

On his way to the dueling grounds, Stephen Decatur probably rode down Pennsylvania Avenue, up and around Jenkins Hill, on which the Capitol was being built, and out what is now Maryland Avenue to the Bladensburg Road. The dueling grounds were just across the District line, past what is now Fort Lincoln Cemetery. They are identified by a historical marker that stands along Maryland State Route 450. The large concrete highway was just a stage route from the capital to Baltimore when the grounds were being used for duels.

Today, ghosts still walk here, even though not much of the original ground remains. Several of the giant trees are survivors of that era, and I cannot help but wonder what secrets they would tell if they could talk. More than fifty duels were fought here. The famous and not so famous were among the antagonists who dueled in Bladensburg. Some men hired professional duelists to fill in for them.

Death seemed to hover permanently over Bladensburg, and often to seriously scar even the survivors. The duelists who walked away from those bloody grounds had seen death, and often their lives were drastically changed. One *Washington Star* writer of the 1890's recalled how some "appeared to be as walking corpses." This seemed particularly true in cases where the duels were fought at close range.

One of the shades that haunts the Bladensburg dueling grounds is suspected of being a party to a tragic encounter that occurred in February of 1819. A former Virginia senator, General Armistead T. Mason, was challenged by his cousin Colonel John M. McCarty. Some accounts said the cousins quarreled over a woman, some attributed it to a dispute over Mason's right to vote in a Leesburg, Virginia, election.

Colonel McCarty felt the only way to settle the feud was by a means that would allow neither to escape. What more sure-fire way than to leap from the top of the new Capitol building? Mason would have no part of it. The Colonel importuned Mason to join him atop a lighted keg of powder. Mason told McCarty he was insane. McCarty countered with charges of cowardice. At the same time, he tossed out an offer to fight at ten paces with muskets filled with buckshot. Mason liked the odds better, but felt they could still be improved. He suggested that a single ball replace the buckshot, and that the duel be held at twelve paces. McCarty hurried home to prepare his musket.

The sun's first rays were shining through the barren trees as the men met at Bladensburg Tavern. It was a familiar scene on the mornings of bloodletting: the two groups of adversaries were gathered at opposite corners of the tavern, seconds and friends filling the ears of the combatants with encouragement and advice. Finally, it was time to venture out into the cold. It was a bleak morning. No birds could be heard, just Blood Run trickling along a narrow winding gully by the edge of the field. The men positioned themselves. A second barked the count.

Two shots rang out.

Mason fell dead.

McCarty was struck in the hand, and the bullet traveled up the muscle of his arm and out his shoulder. McCarty had his "honor," but he had lost the ability to use his right arm. In the years that followed, he tried to put that February morning out of his mind. Friends said that the pain would not allow it. Over and over in McCarty's mind he replayed the scene, heard the shots, and felt the pain as it moved up his arm. Repeatedly he saw Mason fall dead.

Some fifty years later, a newspaper writer looked back on the aftermath of that duel. He wrote that after the duel, McCarty's behavior became erratic, causing him "to become a wanderer." His deep depression made him apathetic about his appearance. The article said that he often was seen in wrinkled clothing, looking "unkempt."

Some wonder if one of the wispy corpses seen walking in a trancelike state over the old dueling ground is not McCarty's tortured soul still searching for his cousin, or the life his cousin had robbed him of when he sent that bullet up McCarty's arm.

Another of the shades often silhouetted against the moonlight as it roams the old grounds could be that of young Daniel Key—son of the author of "The Star-Spangled Banner," Francis Scott Key. Young Daniel argued with a midshipman friend, John Sherburne, over the speed of two steamboats. Some say it was the tension of a long sea voyage that led the two Annapolis students to argue, but nevertheless they could hardly wait to be put ashore to settle their discord on the field of honor.

After visiting their families, the young men met at Bladensburg. Young Key never celebrated his twenty-first birthday. A brilliant and promising career in the Navy was snuffed out with a single shot under the June sun in 1836.

As more and more blood was shed in the name of honor, the public became aroused about dueling. Stories about the moans and groans and darkened apparitions stalking the fog-shrouded grounds began to spread. Gradually, people started to show concern over the continuation of this legal killing.

112   One of the main drawbacks to outlaw-
ing dueling was the lack of uniformity in
the laws. The Maryland antidueling law
did not cover residents of the District of
Columbia or other states; and in the District, so many congressmen believed in
the dueling code that they were reluctant
to outlaw what they considered the
manly art of self-defense. An incident in
February of 1838, however, finally
caused such a public outcry that Congress was forced to act.

Popular Congressman Jonathan Cilley
of Maine was shot to death by Congressman William Graves of Kentucky, who
was a stand-in for New York newspaper
editor James W. Webb. Cilley had called
Webb corrupt. Graves was a good friend
of Webb's and took the charge personally. He felt that a remark against Webb
was a remark against him.

Graves knew weapons and was an experienced marksman. Cilley knew nothing
about guns, let alone dueling. The thirty-
eight-year-old congressman had a wife
and three children, took his work seriously, and tried to serve his district well.
He seemed to try to put the challenge
from Graves out of his mind. Some said
that he never really expected it to come
down to two grown men actually firing
shots at each other. Graves, on the other
hand, engaged in target practice for
weeks before the duel.

On the cold winter morning agreed to
by both parties, Graves showed up with
a rifle much more powerful than the one
Cilley brought. He was allowed to use it,
though. The seconds helped position the
pair eighty paces apart. The count was
shouted. Shots were exchanged, but no
one was struck.

The bizarre scene was repeated, but
again the results were the same. The seconds wanted both to agree they were satisfied, but Graves would not consider the
request until they fired one more round.

In the third round, Cilley's left leg was
shot out from under him. The bullet
from Graves's high-powered rifle tore
into a large artery in Cilley's left leg, and
within ninety seconds life had ebbed
from the body of the young, likable congressman from Maine. Several members
from the House and Senate watched . . .
in silence.

*Representative Jonathan Cilley from Maine,
a reluctant participant in a fatal duel, is just
one of the victims whose spirits visit
the old dueling grounds.*

Congressman Cilley had not yet been
laid to rest in Congressional Cemetery
when the public protest began. The
tragic end of Jonathan Cilley so outraged
Washington that the next session of Congress was forced to make dueling—or
accepting or giving a challenge—a crimi-
nal offense within the District of Columbia.

The law appeased the public but unfortunately did not put an end to
dueling. The challenges were made less
openly, and the "meets" became more
clandestine. Finally, the outbreak of the
Civil War brought an end to the deadly
dawn ritual so often staged at Bladensburg. After the war, things were not the
same. The carnage of war had taken the
sport out of killing.

The old inn located near the dueling
grounds saw only a fraction of the business it had enjoyed in earlier years when
men of courage would stop in for a toast,
and men without courage would come by
for some out of a bottle. The inn folded
long ago, but it is in the process of being
restored. Not so the dueling grounds,
however. The fields around the old
grounds have been overtaken by sprawl-

More than fifty duels were fought at the infamous Bladensburg dueling grounds, seen in the background beyond the creek, then called Blood Run. The spirits of those who died here come back to haunt the spot, even today.

ing urban growth that has choked off all but a tiny corner of those infamous grounds. A few towering trees shade what's left of the grass, but an asphalt playground covers the rest of the open space. "Blood Run," or "Dueling Creek," has been renamed once more, but "Eastern Branch" just doesn't have the same ring to it. There is a high chain-link fence around the stream to guard the children from contact with its polluted waters. Not too many children play there after dusk. You don't see too many adults crossing the site of the old dueling grounds at night either. Newspaper boys skirt the area, which often is misty early in the morning, afraid of what they might see in the first light. Those who have had occasion to walk across it have often told of fog-shrouded shadows of men of another era.

One youth who reported a dramatic encounter with one such spirit described it to his father as "dark, but not really transparent.

Like a man dressed in black, an old man, whose back was bowed and head cast downward," the boy said. He saw it for only a few seconds before he stepped on a twig that snapped. The noise apparently caused the apparition to vanish. There is no answer to what it is that causes these doomed men to revisit the field where they died in defense of honor, for at the slightest sound they fade, leaving no time for questions— should any one be brave enough to try to ask one.

THE RESTLESS VAMPIRE

As preposterous as it sounds, a vampire once visited the Nation's Capital and left its identifying marks on several victims. The largest newspaper coverage of the story occurred just a few years after the novel *Dracula* was published in this country.

Legend has it that a young girl from a well-respected family fell in love with a handsome European prince with piercing black eyes whom she had met at a party at an unnamed embassy. He concealed the fact that he was a vampire until he got her alone one evening—under a full moon. The young girl's pale body was found early the next morning at the edge of a clearing not too many miles from her home. The mark of the vampire on her neck was obscured by her long flowing hair.

Some say that the fine lace the young woman was laid to rest in had been intended for a wedding dress. She was sealed in her family's burial vault, and flowers were laid over the stone slab, but having once received the bite of the vampire, she too would rise again as a vampire. Apparently finished with his recruiting in Washington, the prince was never reported to have been seen again.

In the 1920's, Gorman Hendricks was given considerable space in the *Washington Post* to tell about a "white-clad beautiful girl" whose face was "distorted by a pair of wolf-like fangs." Hendricks said that a vampire had bitten her in the 1850's and then proceeded to tell what had happened to her since.

The first chilling encounter apparently occurred within weeks or months of the young girl's death. The article says that a woodcutter making his way home "spotted a white-robed figure of a woman floating through the sealed vault." Nobody believed him until a stable groom's lifeless body was found a few months later. This time the mark of the vampire did not escape detection. Remembering the woodcutter's tale, people became panic-stricken. Out came the garlic bags to ward off vampire attacks. The neighbors were terrified that the creature might return, so they also put a couple of heavily armed men in front of the burial vault around the clock. Hendricks said that the watch was maintained for many nights before the night stalker put in another appearance.

It was on the "eve of St. George" during a thunderstorm that two dozing guards were awakened by what sounded to them like the squeak of rusty iron hinges. According to one eyewitness, a figure crept out "and glided through the woods in the direction of the mansion." Apparently the men didn't stick around to see if she went in. They seemed anxious to get back to the neighbors with their news. Next morning, well after the sun brightly lit the way, a small group of brave but frightened people cautiously ventured back out to the old estate to investigate. At the tomb they found that "the huge stone slab over the coffin had been displaced." Hendricks said that the girl was in the coffin, but "sharp wolf-like fangs" that parted her blood-red lips sent a ripple of shudders and gasps through the group. He said that they thought to fasten the coffin lid before running, but made no mention of anyone driving a stake through her heart. Perhaps that is why reports of her ghost stalking the neighborhood persisted.

Hendricks described another encounter a few months later. A man ran into the spirit as it floated through the trees near the vine-covered and "half-forgotten vault." The man told the reporter that the creature was emitting a maniacal laugh and claimed that he caught "the foul odor of the charnel house and saw the gleam of hell-fire" in the thing's eyes. The man must have been in terrible shape after that encounter for Hendricks says that he died a week later.

Legend has it that the neighbors didn't want the family in the neighborhood, so to avoid possible violence the family moved away. News of the vampire spread throughout the area and nobody would buy the house of a vampire's family. It remained deserted for quite a while, and according to Hendricks, decay had set in before someone unfamiliar with the old stories moved in.

Fresh blood in the old house was apparently something the vampire couldn't resist. The new occupants reported a horrible figure "gazing in the window of an upper room," and then moved out. Neighbors, who several times in the past had thought they were rid of the vampire, found themselves reaching for the garlic again. Petrified, they shunned the property day and night, and when it stormed no one ventured outside. When Hendricks wrote the article in 1923, he described the vault's door as hanging on "rusty hinges," adding that "the hand of time has obliterated the name." Hendricks described "large sections of broken sandstone that once covered the tombs of the dead" that, he said, "lie about the dank vault given over to the creatures that creep and crawl."

The legend spanned a century, and the last reported victims were those mentioned in Hendricks's story. If there have been none since, the vigilantes have succeeded, but I suppose it could be argued that in a bustling international city twice the size of Hendricks's town, not many people are going to take the time to raise a question about two tiny red perforations on a few necks now and then.

THE PHANTOM OF THE NATIONAL THEATRE

The National Theatre, near 13th and E Streets, Northwest, was built in the 1830's. Its illustrious history includes many of this country's most notable theatrical events and many of America's finest Thespians have strutted and fretted their hours upon that stage. Yet, to my knowledge, only one actor from a bygone era still regularly visits the theater.

It seems that the actor was slain by an insanely jealous fellow actor who buried his body in the basement under the stage. Whether they had argued over a pretty young actress or over who would have the most lines in the new play cannot be answered.

The old basement is off-limits except to certain key theater personnel. I tried, unsuccessfully, on several occasions during the past few years to gain permission to have a look downstairs and question at least one stage watchman who has actually had an encounter with the old actor. I did manage to talk by phone with the old man, but he became edgy and upset when he learned that I knew he had once spotted the apparition. Under no circumstances would he discuss the encounter.

According to the legend, the old actor generally makes himself visible near the prompter's table whenever a new show is being readied. He is said to look around, inspect the sets, indicate his approval or disapproval—and vanish.

The old boy has never spoken to anyone as far as I could learn, but one thing is certain: those around the National Theatre have virtually adopted the ghost as a mascot and are very protective of him.

SOME HAUNTS OF MARY SURRATT

The Old Brick Capitol isn't the only location still frequented by Mary Surratt. Her spirit has also been reported drifting around the grounds where the old Arsenal Penitentiary once stood. It was there in the courtyard on the northern end of Fort Lesley McNair not too far from Capitol Hill that she and three of the other conspirators were hanged. Their bodies were buried near the gallows, and then later moved to permanent graves.

There is an old tale that Mary Surratt's spirit had considerable influence over the sudden appearance of a boxwood tree that seemingly grew of its own accord to mark the site of the scaffold. It is claimed that this is her way of continuing to attract attention to prove her innocence.

Several old newspapers quote some soldiers as saying that there is another spirit that comes to the picturesque old fort, whose grounds slope into the Washington Channel of the Potomac. Walter Reed, the conqueror of typhoid and yellow fevers, had not yet begun his medical schooling, which would eventually take him to Fort McNair, when Mary Surratt and the other Lincoln conspirators were executed. However, the famed doctor, who died unexpectedly of appendicitis shortly after he freed Cuba from yellow fever, has reportedly been seen strolling the grounds of the old fort, where he served as a professor at the Army Medical School. Those soldiers who claim to have seen his bespectacled ghost say that it walks slowly, head down, hands folded behind its back. Some think Reed—or his spirit—appears to be concentrating on what further benefit he could have been to mankind had not death so rudely snatched him away from life.

One cannot help but wonder what would happen if the spirits of Dr. Reed and Mrs. Surratt ever met. One of the soldiers I asked about the old tales said, "Them two may haunt this place, but I got a damn good hunch they report back to different quarters."

The troubled spirit of Mary Surratt

just can't seem to find a place to rest. Some have seen it wandering around her old home off Brandywine Road in nearby Clinton, Maryland. Others swear that her spirit is responsible for strange noises that have been reported inside what used to be her boarding house in the 600 block of H Street, Northwest.

In the fertile tobacco lands of southern Maryland, just east of Washington, Mary Jenkins married John Surratt. It was 1835. President Andrew Jackson had narrowly escaped assassination during a war with the Seminoles. Mary and John Surratt weren't concerned. Politics were in Washington and that was a lifetime away. They were newlyweds and had a twelve-hundred-acre farm to run. There weren't many neighbors then, but as the years passed more and more people seemed to settle in the area. Within fifteen years John and Mary decided that they would turn part of the Surratt house into a country store and tavern. Folks used to drop by often, and they even began calling the town Surrattsville. The area kept that name for more than a dozen years—even after John died and Mary, having leased the property to a former District policeman, took her two children to Washington to escape all those memories.

Ford's Theatre wasn't too far from Mary's new home; neither were the other theaters and the White House. It was a convenient place for John Wilkes Booth, an actor from a family of actors, to seek lodging. It would offer him the seclusion he sought in directing and casting his real-life play.

At midnight on the night Lincoln was shot, police and federal troops rousted Mary Surratt out of bed, accused her of being a conspirator, and took her off to prison in the Old Brick Capitol. Her insistence of innocence and her denial that she knew Booth well fell on ears disciplined not to listen.

An article in the *Washington Star* stated that she was never even allowed a change of clothes. She was "forced to wear the same garments in which she was arrested until hanged July 7, 1865."

Within a few years after her death, there were hints that something strange was going on at her former H Street house. Daughter Annie had sold the old boarding house for less than half its value not long after her mother's execution. After that, the turnover in owners was so rapid that it attracted the attention of journalists of the period, who began to chronicle the tales former owners sometimes told *after* they had rid themselves of the property. Most of the accounts dealt with "ominous sounds," "mumblings," or "muffled sounds." Some claimed "muffled whispers" rehearsed again "the dastardly plot." The creaking of boards on the second floor was supposedly caused by the specter of Mary Surratt, who is doomed to an eternity of walking Washington until her name is cleared.

The Surratt boarding house has been renovated inside and out many times, and is currently serving as a Chinese grocery store. After several years there, the owner has no complaints.

But the spirit of Mary Surratt isn't resting. For instance, it has been reported back in her old farmhouse-tavern in what is now Clinton. Folks there didn't want to call their community Surrattsville after Mary was hanged. You see, it had been the former Washington policeman-turned-tavern-keeper who had turned her in. Booth is said to have stopped by her Clinton house for supplies and food as he tried to elude his pursuers before crossing over into Virginia. He was captured twelve days later in Bowling Green when troopers set fire to the barn in which he was hiding after he refused to come out. Whether he was shot or killed himself can still ignite a good debate.

Some say that Mary Surratt's ghost returns to that old frame house in Clinton with the wide front porch to relive all those years she shared there with John. Others, though, have said that her return is motivated by her strong desire to find the tavern keeper who turned her in.

Mary Surratt, here pictured with other conspirators convicted of the plot to assassinate Abraham Lincoln, is still supposed to be roaming Washington in her unceasing effort to clear her name.

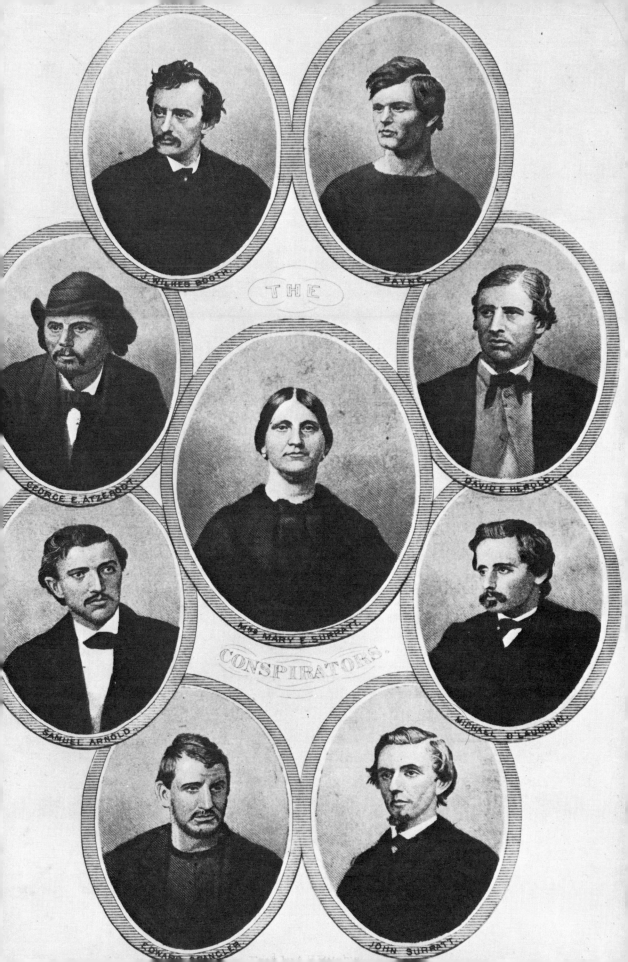

118

*Mary Surratt's former boarding house at
604 H Street, Northwest, is one of the places
her spirit has been seen.*

*Another haunt of Mary Surratt's restless spirit
is the Washington Arsenal, now Fort Leslie
McNair, where she was hanged.*

THE GAMBLER

During the middle part of the last century, one of Washington's legendary gamblers was Colonel Beau Hickman. Local lore has it that he was easily recognized by his beaver hat, cane, and penchant for diamond pins. One article said that Beau was about twenty when he left his Virginia home in 1833 to come to Washington, seeking fame and fortune in the big city. His good looks and his gift for handling a deck of cards convinced him that he would succeed.

For some forty years, Hickman lived in Washington—spending most of his time in the old hotel that was located at 6th Street and Pennsylvania Avenue, Northwest. The Colonel provided many men of the city with pleasurable times—or in quite a few instances—unpleasurable times. It all depended on which way the cards fell. Even when the cards didn't fall just right for his friends, the Colonel seemed most adroit at soothing

their losses with good liquor and beautiful women. Gamblers seldom have friends, but Colonel Beau proved to be the exception, and nothing more illustrated this fact than his own death.

Newspapers tell us that in 1873 some of his card-playing friends were startled to learn of the Colonel's sudden death through a small obituary in the newspaper, and even more shocked to read that burial was in the pauper's graveyard. Never in their wildest dreams had his friends imagined the Colonel penniless.

After the initial shock passed, the group gathered in the saloon of the hotel where the Colonel had lived. They reminisced about the many hours of pleasure the Colonel had provided them. None expressed any bitterness toward the old gambler, which may explain why he died broke. The Colonel never fleeced his friends.

With moist eyes and spirits warmed with alcohol, the gentlemen decided that their long-time host deserved a more prominent resting place. It just wouldn't

---

Dr. Walter Reed's spirit is also said to walk the grounds of the old Arsenal, brooding about his work, which was cut short by his premature death.

be right for such a fine fellow to spend eternity in a pauper's grave. Such a noble person should be buried in Congressional Cemetery, they reasoned. So, after one last drink for the road, the men set out for the pauper's field. Dusk was settling as they arrived at the deserted cemetery on the outskirts of Washington, but there was enough light for them to see that body snatchers had been at work.

It wasn't a particularly reputable occupation—as a matter of fact it was illegal —but a good living could be made selling cadavers to "no-questions-asked" medical schools. Shuddering with fear, the men saw the Colonel's body lying half in and half out of the freshly reopened grave. Someone had frightened off the body snatchers. The Colonel's friends went quickly to work. Turning their faces into the wind, taking a deep breath, and closing their eyes, the men grabbed up the body in its shroud and tossed it into the back of their wagon. With the crack of a whip, and an obscene shout, they were off to a greener and more respectable gravesite in Congressional Cemetery. The Colonel's body bounced around in the buckboard as it flew along G Street. It looked as though that old wagon was being chased by the

devil himself. The wagon nearly tipped over as the horses galloped through the gates of Congressional Cemetery and around the curve to where the Colonel would be reburied. The grave was dug, the Colonel was lowered into it, prayed over, and covered up in less than an hour. One chronicler of the tale says that one of the men even produced a thin marble tombstone with no markings on it. With a piece of burned wood, he scribbled the Colonel's name and the date of his death. Tipping their hats in one final gesture of respect, the men jumped onto the wagon and in a cloud of dust headed back for the old hotel on Pennsylvania Avenue.

Reportedly, the Colonel never forgave his friends for their cowardice and their mockery of such a solemn occasion. That is said to be part of the reason why he visits the area of 6th and Pennsylvania Avenue, Northwest. Not long after the Colonel's death, people began to tell tales of wild things happening in some of the card games at the old hotel—particularly card games involving the Colonel's old friends.

The Colonel's spirit liked a joke as well as the Colonel had. He even got to one of his friends at a most tender moment during his courtship of a beautiful young woman. Yes, the Colonel was dead, but his spirit was dedicated to making sure that his friends wouldn't forget him.

The Colonel's old hotel was torn down in 1892 to make way for the new Atlantic Coastline Railroad Headquarters, but that apparently had little effect on the Colonel's spirit. Once a gambler, always a gambler, and the Colonel has been seen standing on his corner just after dark, wearing a rather lonely expression as he searches for his friends and just one more game.

Those claiming to have spotted Colonel Beau say you can't mistake him. He's still wearing his beaver hat, his cane, and a diamond stickpin.

AN UNSUCCESSFUL EXORCISM

In September of 1907 the *Washington Star* carried a story about an attempted exorcism in a house at 11th and D Streets, Northwest. If we are to believe the article, the owner had a great deal of trouble renting the property, described as "a fine old home." The writer says that the owner was reluctant to believe the many stories of supernatural occurrences his tenants had told, but he was finally convinced that something had to be done. When all attempts at ridding the house of the unwelcome presence had failed, he consulted his parish priest. The writer was quite vague about the exact nature of the troubles that caused the owner to seek an exorcist, yet the details of the attempted exorcism, and who attempted it, are carefully spelled out.

The reporter said that the owner talked with "Father Boyle and an assistant priest of St. Patrick's Church" about performing the ancient rite of exorcism. The reporter says that the priests, though at first reluctant, gave in because of the desperation of the owner of the house. Father Boyle and his assistant arrived at the deserted home, just off Pennsylvania Avenue, at precisely 11 P.M. They went through the house turning on all the gaslights, and closing and bolting the heavy wooden shutters, windows, and doors. We are told that they established themselves in the exact center of the house, and I would have been disappointed if the reporter had not noted that the hallway timepiece chimed twelve as they prepared to begin the exorcism.

Suddenly, locked windows flew open, shutters banged against the side of the house, and doors opened and closed. The writer says, "The iron bar across the front door was lifted by invisible hands" and slammed to the floor. Wailing and screaming began to fill the rooms.

Like most articles of the period, this one is melodramatic, but it conjures up a picture of the priest and his assistant trying to shout the words of their ritual over the sobbing and wailing that echoed through first one room and then another as the distraught spirit searched for those who threatened it. The priests apparently saw nothing, yet they knew they had encountered something not of this world. Strong winds of gale force and maniacal laughter shook the inside of the house, and created such a tempest that pieces of furniture toppled over and were blown about as though made of cardboard. It is possible that the priest and his assistant were overcome with a feeling that the wind was actually compelling them through the doorway and out of the house.

The writer said that they were unable to complete the rite that evening, but had sufficiently recovered the next day to apologize to the owner of the house and to promise to return the following evening to try again. Noting that the owner was a reasonable man, the reporter inferred that he decided that any spirit capable of defying men of God must be truly evil. Rather than risk the lives of the priests by further attempts, the owner decided to have the house torn down— hoping to put an end to the horrifying events for all time.

The owner was no doubt relieved that his decision restored calm to the neigh-

DRIPS OF GORE!

A Horrible Sort of Ghost That Haunts a House on 19th Street.

WASHINGTON IS THE GREATEST TOWN for ghosts in this country. The city is dotted all over with haunted houses which remain unrented year after year on account of the spooks that are supposed to inhabit them, all the way from the great empty Tayloe mansion at the corner of 17th street and New York avenue to the humble and deserted negro hut in Swampoodle, regarded by neighborhood superstition as the abode of bogies most horrible and frightening.

But perhaps the most thoroughly original of Washington ghosts is located in a house on 19th street northwest between E and R. The dwelling has been for rent and unoccupied nearly all of the time for several years past, notwithstanding its situation in the fashionable quarter. The last tenants were induced to take it by the extremely low rent, although the real estate agent, for security's sake, would only let them have it on a year's lease. How they got out of the bargain I don't know, but they moved away at the end of the fifth week. That was six months ago.

It seems that eight years ago a man committed suicide in this house with a razor. The deed was done in cold blood apparently. He stood in front of the mirror which overhung the marble mantelpiece and deliberately cut his throat from ear to ear. Then, as appeared from the condition in which things were subsequently found, he clung with one hand to the mantelpiece, while his blood poured out upon the hearth, until he fell and died.

That was the story, as the tenants here referred to understood it afterward. Their notion of the ghost when they took the house was altogether indefinite, and they only laughed at it, considering it rather in the light of a joke than otherwise. It so chanced that what, as they found out later, was reputed to be the particular haunted chamber was occupied by the two daughters of the family—fifteen and eighteen years of age respectively.

From first to last there was no such thing observed as an apparition. The girls slept well, save for the fact that they were annoyed on occasions by a sound of dripping, which they at first supposed was caused by a leak of some sort. But their surprise was awakened by the continuance of this dripping during a long spell of dry weather, and more particularly did they find reason at length for wonderment in the circumstance that the dripping began invariably at about 11:15 p. m. and lasted for perhaps twenty minutes, but not longer.

The dripping sound seemed to come from the mantelpiece and they carefully investigated that fixture and its surroundings, but without result, save for the discovery of a slightly hollowed area in the stone underneath, which had apparently been made by scraping away its substance.

Inquiry developed the fact that the stone had been scraped away for the purpose of eliminating the spot where a pool of the suicide's blood had formed. Also it was learned that the hour at which he killed himself was about 11:15 p.m.

The tenants moved out.

borhood, for years rolled by and no one has heard anything more about strange happenings from 11th and D, Northwest.

THE SATISFIED POLTERGEIST

Let's return to H Street, Northwest, where tales of another haunt appeared in an old newspaper story. This one happened around the turn of the century in a house on H Street near 18th Street, Northwest. The story concerned a family that had been victims of an old servant's pesky poltergeist. It seems that the servant died without telling anyone about the cash she had stashed beneath her mattress, which she had been saving to help a cousin come North.

The article described strange occurrences in her former room—"stomping sounds that would awake the soundest of sleepers," chairs that rocked mysteriously, blankets and quilts that flew off the bed whenever someone tried to sleep on it. If we are to believe that old article, the servant was so determined to help her relative that her spirit kept coming back to lead someone to the treasure.

The owners of the haunted house decided that the room was of no value as a bedroom, and determined to see what would happen if they converted it to a sewing room. In dismantling the bedroom, one of their first steps was to remove the mattress from the bed. An envelope bearing the name and address of the servant's cousin fell onto the floor. Everyone lived happily ever after, according to the reporter. The money was forwarded to the needy relative, the servant's spirit was allowed to rest, and the family was overjoyed at the return of peace and quiet.

This article published in the Washington Star *of April 18, 1891, is typical of the newspaper coverage of ghost stories at that time.*

THE TAILOR'S SLAIN BRIDE

Another tale of passion, violence, and death concerned a home on I Street, Northwest—just off Connecticut Avenue and yet still near Lafayette Square.

The tale goes back to the 1870's, when, legend has it, a rather successful tailor moved into the home with his bride. The writer of one of the articles I read said that he seemed quite proud at having been able to afford such a home so near to where some of the city's notables lived and worked. It wasn't too long after they moved in that neighbors began to notice that the bride never came outside. Even when people called on the couple, they were greeted only by the tailor, who seemed distant, though cordial. Inquiries about his bride drew casual remarks and a quick change of subject. He is said to have mentioned that she was "visiting relatives," and turned the conversation in other directions.

As busybody neighbors spread the rumor that the bride had left her husband, and amused themselves by speculating why, the tailor moved out of his house, never to be seen in the neighborhood again.

Most of the neighbors just figured that he had joined his wife in the city of her relatives. It wasn't until new occupants began to turn over rather frequently that some people began to suspect that the man had murdered his wife. Gossips used to say that was the only way to explain the moans and the rapping sounds from within the walls that sometimes kept the house vacant for months.

One determined occupant felt that all the house needed was a good remodeling. The article I read pictured him as a skeptic and not at all convinced that a ghost was causing his problems. He believed that the moans were from a brisk wind blowing through loose window and door frames. You can imagine his surprise when he knocked down one of the walls and as the plaster dust settled, found a skeleton. A wedding ring encircled one finger bone, and there was a silver letter opener lodged between two bones in the rib cage. Blowing away the plaster dust, the man found that the blade was stained a deep crimson.

One article on the old house said that the uncovering of the skeleton of the tailor's wife unleashed an awesome volume of stories, which only served to keep the house unoccupied over longer periods.

One such story revolved around a shadowy woman, dressed in white, who often stalked the rooms—mumbling a name no one could understand. Harm had never come to anyone who had lived in the home since the tailor left it, and apparently the stories were not taken too

Navy Secretary Benjamin Tracy ignored stories of a woman in white said to haunt the house at 1634 I Street, Northwest, and moved in with his wife.

seriously by Benjamin Tracy and his wife when they moved in, in the 1890's. Tracy was Benjamin Harrison's newly appointed Secretary of the Navy. Many think that Benjamin Tracy would have been better off if he had paid some attention to the old tales. For the fire that consumed the house not too many months later killed Tracy's beloved wife.

Although fire officials claimed otherwise, there were those who were convinced that the fire was the work of the spirit, who out of desperation at not finding her slayer in any part of the house during the decades she had been searching, caused the fire in order to free her frustrated soul to continue its search for the tailor elsewhere.

THE CURSE OF THE HOPE DIAMOND

The specter of a nude woman, described by some as of "unparalleled beauty and form," is said to occasionally grace the imposing stairway inside the palatial Indonesian Embassy at 2020 Massachusetts Avenue, Northwest. Those who keep the lore of Embassy Row alive like to think that it is a youthful Evalyn Walsh McLean visiting the home she first occupied upon coming East—a home where she had known only happiness. All of that, of course, was before she and her husband, Ned, acquired the infamous Hope Diamond.

Evalyn Walsh first met Edward McLean in Denver when he was covering the Democratic Convention for his father's newspaper. The 1908 election went to Republican William Howard Taft, but politics was the furthest thing from the minds of Evalyn and Ned. They were married that year, and celebrated by leaving the country for "a happy whirlwind of worldwide travels," as one newspaper article described their honeymoon. Evalyn Walsh was the daughter of a western miner who had struck it rich, and Edward McLean was heir to the *Washington Post*. It was while the McLeans were in Turkey that Evalyn first saw the most seductive gem she had ever laid her eyes on. She was totally captivated by the shimmering blue diamond on the neck of a sultan's harem favorite, and never really put it from her mind. In 1922 when she heard that the sultan had been dethroned and his favorite wife murdered, she set out to acquire the stone.

The fact that the sultan's life fell apart when he came into possession of the Hope Diamond didn't seem to bother Evalyn McLean. She told reporters shortly after acquiring the stone that she never believed any of the stories of tragedy and death connected with it. There were whispers, however, that she discouraged her friends from touching it and never allowed her children to. And for one who did not believe those sinister stories, many thought it strange that Evalyn arranged a ceremony in which a priest blessed the diamond. One reporter

Evalyn Walsh McLean continued to flout the curse of the Hope Diamond, even after May Yohe, whose husband once owned the stone, wrote to warn her. May Yohe said the diamond had ruined her life and urged Ev to throw it away and break its spell.

said that the guests at the ceremony became rather unnerved when a storm broke out and lightning flashed through the windows as the priest performed the rites.

Centuries before, the Hope Diamond was supposed to have been part of the 112-carat eye of an Indian idol. The diamond had been stolen and sold to a man named Tavernier, whom some have described as a French adventurer. He smuggled it into Paris, but not long after, he met a slow and horrible death as the victim of a pack of wild dogs. Later, the stone turned up as part of the French royal jewels, although Louis XIV probably wished that he had never acquired the diabolical diamond. Legend has it that his eldest son, his eldest grandson, and his great-grandson fell victim to the curse within a year. History documents that his trusted confidant, Nicholas Fou-

quet, who had once worn the stone, fell from grace and was executed. The Princess de Lamballe, who had dared to wear it, was murdered by a mob. Stanley Loomis theorizes in *The Fatal Friendship,* written in 1973, that the diamond was used to bribe the commander of a foreign army to leave France after he had brought his troops near Paris to save the imprisoned Louis XVI and Marie Antoinette.

The royal couple lost their heads, and the stone, too, was lost for quite a while. The next place it surfaced was in Amsterdam, where a jeweler named Fals recut it. Those who believe the legend say that the new shape and size did not affect the curse. They relate how Fals's own son stole the diamond from him and years later when Fals died poor and broken in spirit, took his own life out of guilt for what he had done to his father.

Tragedy also touched the life of Edward McLean, seen here (on the right) with good friend Warren G. Harding. His marriage fell apart, his drinking problem grew worse, he was declared insane and hospitalized for eight years before he died of a heart attack.

This house at 2020 Massachusetts Avenue once belonged to Evalyn Walsh McLean and is now the Indonesian Embassy. Even today a nude apparition, said to be the spirit of a youthful Evalyn McLean searching for the happy days she had spent there, is seen on the stairway.

In 1830, Henry Thomas Hope, a London banker, acquired what was reported in one newspaper article to be "a 45-carat sapphire-blue diamond." From this point on the stone bore Hope's name. The curse spared him, but not his grandson. After inheriting the diamond, the young man soon found his own marriage to American actress Mae Yohe on the rocks. He died poor and his former wife eventually fared no better. Her career collapsed and she too died after several poverty-stricken years. According to the legend, the Hope Diamond next made its way into Russia, where it was acquired by Catherine the Great. Her life of turbulence, marital woes, and death by apoplexy is well known.

As a new century dawned, the curse of the Hope Diamond remained strong. A merchant in gems and precious stones acquired it in Turkey for a wealthy sultan who sought to impress his harem favorite. The merchant delivered the goods but never lived long enough to enjoy his share of the sale. He, his wife, and their children were killed in a terrible accident in which their car crashed down a deep precipice.

Now, Evalyn Walsh McLean had the diamond, and when the priest concluded his blessing, a collective sigh of relief could be heard from the few guests present. The Hope Diamond was returned to its place of safekeeping, and some even say the storm quieted down.

Two of the first people to handle the Hope Diamond after Evalyn acquired it were her mother-in-law and a friend of her mother-in-law, Mrs. Robert Goelet. In her book *Father Struck It Rich,* Evalyn McLean says, "Within a narrow space, just about a year or so, both women died."

In spite of the constant protection Evalyn Walsh McLean gave her son, Vinson, he was only nine years old when he died in an accident.

As the years passed, Evalyn Walsh McLean continued to insist to reporters that she was not a believer in the curse, yet the press was filled with stories about how protective she was of her young son Vinson. Often there were pictures. One article featured a photograph of young Vinson in a goat cart being pulled around his mother's elaborate new estate, Friendship, just off Wisconsin Avenue at R Street, Northwest. One writer said that the boy had six automobiles assigned to him, and he was always driven by a chauffeur "in order that he might not run the risk of accident and contamination that might result from riding in other persons' cars." There was a complete staff to protect Vinson. Some speculated that Evalyn lived in fear of a Lindbergh-type kidnapping. It was widely reported in the Washington press when she hired the entire circus to come to her estate rather than take the little boy to the circus.

Vinson had always been showered with everything money could buy. The year after his mother acquired the Hope Diamond, one newspaper reporter wrote that his Christmas presents cost $40,000, and that "they included a working model

of the Gatun locks on the Panama Canal and a miniature steam yacht." Money, however, could not give Vinson a long life. When he was nine years old, the curse penetrated the protection: an out-of-control automobile struck Vinson McLean in front of his home.

Evalyn McLean's marriage was becoming stormy. Their bickerings at parties attracted attention and often made the society pages, but Evalyn and her husband continued to entertain often and lavishly. One society reporter wrote about friends "close to the McLeans" who privately expressed opinions that the pair liked crowds because they had grown to dislike each other's company so much.

The parties gave the town's newspapers something to write about. Often, reporters listed the scores of notables present; several tried to pin down rumors that some of the garden parties featured nudes on pedestals; others concentrated on the political aspects of the affairs.

Warren G. Harding was a good friend of the McLeans', and Ned worked on the Harding Inaugural Committee. The election of 1920 had been a great success for Harding, but the legend surrounding the Hope Diamond would have us believe that Harding's life began to change after he came in contact with the diamond. His health declined and he began to suffer from heart, lung, and stomach trouble. In 1922, two men in his administration died violently. One shot himself to death, the other either committed suicide or was murdered—amid charges that they had fattened their bank accounts at government expense. In 1923, Harding left Washington for a western tour. His trip left him totally exhausted, and on August 2, he died in San Francisco of what was diagnosed as a blood clot in the brain.

Several months after Harding's death, the Teapot Dome scandal broke wide open. Ned McLean's name was brought up in connection with a $100,000 check

The ill-fated Warren G. Harding, a close friend of Edward and Evalyn McLean, who some say was another victim of the curse of the Hope Diamond.

to Interior Secretary Albert Fall, who had been accused of selling off government oil supplies to Harry Sinclair and Edward Doheny.

Edward McLean's drinking problem grew, and press reports indicate that his wife became less and less tolerant, often berating him in public. Newspaper headlines from the mid twenties to the mid thirties chronicled the McLeans' public fights and separation. Ned tried to divorce Evalyn in Mexico, but she filed a countersuit in this country. According to a *Washington Herald* article in November of 1930, she charged that he had lived "for protracted periods with an unnamed woman; that he drank excessively; and caused Mrs. McLean bodily suffering by beating and striking her, cursing and calling her vile names."

Two years later, when the press reported that Ned had obtained a divorce in Riga, Latvia, Evalyn issued a statement through her attorney that Ned had been hospitalized in Paris for three months "as a result of a complete breakdown," and that the divorce was probably illegal. "There's something decidedly irregular about the whole thing," her statement said.

While Ned was trying to divorce her, she was moving to have him committed to an asylum. "Mrs. McLean Wants Husband Adjudged of Unsound Mind," *Washington Daily News* headlines proclaimed on October 4, 1933. Before the month was over, that newspaper and the others in town reported the verdict of the twenty jurors: McLean was insane. Edward McLean remained hospitalized for eight years before a heart attack added his name to the roster of those whose premature death can be traced to contact with the Hope Diamond.

McLean's death didn't prevent him from still trying to get back at his wife. In July of 1941, the *Washington Daily News* reported that McLean's will "disclosed that in a last dramatic gesture he had cut off his wife with only dower rights and similarly disposed of his children in order to leave $300,000 to Rose Davies . . . his companion in cheerier days."

During that same time, the McLeans' daughter, Evalyn, was making news of

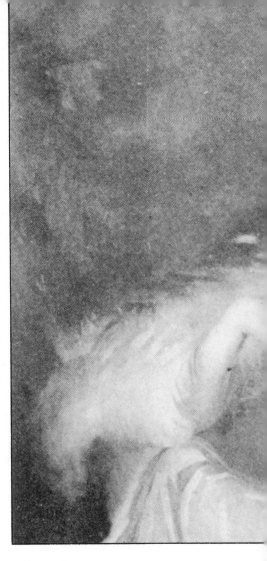

her own. That August one Washington newspaper featured a picture from a few years earlier of North Carolina Senator Robert Rice Reynolds kissing Jean Harlow, and ran another photograph alongside of it of twenty-year-old Evalyn McLean, with her comments on whether or not the fifty-six-year-old "kissing Senator" would marry her.

Although Evalyn Walsh McLean was concerned for her daughter's happiness, she had troubles of her own, which seemed to get worse not better. Newspaper stories were focusing on her willingness to put the Hope Diamond up for collateral for a quarter-of-a-million-dollar loan she needed to help bail the *Washington Post* out of trouble. Evalyn's daughter went on to marry the flamboyant Senator Reynolds, but on September 20, 1946, the fifth wife of the former senator from North Carolina overdosed

Evalyn's daughter, Evalyn Reynolds, also met a tragic death.

on sleeping pills. Evalyn Walsh McLean had survived her husband, her son Vinson, and her only daughter, and like so many of those who have fallen victim to the curse of the stone, her own death was not quick. She fell and broke her hip, and while suffering from that she contracted another illness from which she never recovered.

April 28, 1947, only days after her death, the *Washington Daily News* asked: "Who'll Be the Next to Risk Wearing 'Unlucky' Diamond?"

The Hope Diamond became the property of diamond merchant Harry Winston of New York, who professed that he did not believe in the curse. As the United States entered the fifties, however, the Hope Diamond was placed on what Winston called "permanent loan" to the Smithsonian Institution. One article inferred that he decided to get rid of the stone because his wife kept nagging him to wear it.

The diamond merchant used registered mail to ship the stone from New York to Washington—much to the misfortune of the unsuspecting mail carrier. Soon after delivering the Hope Diamond to the museum, the thirty-five-year-old letter carrier's leg was crushed by a truck. A newspaper article from 1959 reported that within a few months of his encounter with the diamond, the man's wife died of a heart attack, and the family dog hanged itself by jumping from the lawn through an open basement window while still tied to a leash. Nine months after he delivered the diamond, the mailman's suburban Washington home was gutted by fire. Still, in talking to a reporter, he seemed to maintain a rather philosophic attitude about his misfortune. He insisted that he did not believe in the curse of the Hope Diamond: "If the hex is supposed to affect the owners, then the public should be having all the bad luck," he is quoted as saying.

And a case could probably be made that since the government acquired the Hope Diamond and placed it on display in the Smithsonian Institution, our country has fared no better than the letter carrier did. Indeed, neither 2020 Massachusetts Avenue nor Evalyn McLean's later home, Friendship, on Wisconsin Avenue, near R Street, Northwest, seem to be tainted by the curse, so that the satanic stone may very well be concentrating on a much more important victim now.

The Indonesians acquired 2020 Massachusetts Avenue for their embassy several years ago, and it has been fairly quiet except for an occasional encounter with a woman some have glimpsed gliding down the elegant stairway *au naturel.* She is a very popular ghost. It would be a delightful pursuit to learn the identity of the "nocturnal nude," as one reporter called her, but she always seems to vanish before anyone can get close enough to ask her if she was Evalyn Walsh McLean or perhaps another victim of the diamond so strangely misnamed Hope.

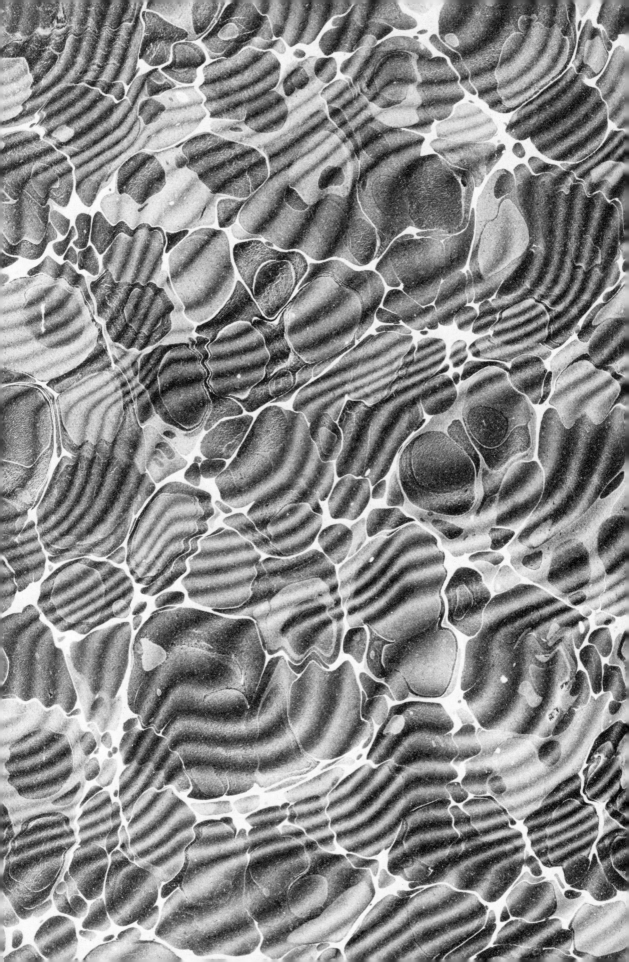

8. OTHER FAMOUS HOUSES

GHOSTS OF THE OCTAGON

The Octagon, at New York Avenue and 18th Streets, Northwest, is a handsome home used by President and Mrs. James Madison while the White House was being rebuilt after the fire of 1814. Dolley Madison's spirit is still spotted there from time to time, and there are tales of other phantom visitors too. Encounters of several types have been reported in newspapers for more than one hundred years. Some involve the great spiral staircase in the entry hall, others have their origins in the dank cellar or subterranean kitchen. Only the United States Capitol and the White House seem to be visited by more ghosts than is this elegant and sturdy home built for Colonel John Tayloe, close friend of George Washington.

Dr. William Thornton, famed for his Capitol building design, built the Octagon for John Tayloe, a Virginia plantation owner, close to where the President's House was being built. It is considered a fine example of Federal architecture. To fit the unusual shape of the lot, the building was designed with six sides (although the Tayloes always called it "The Octagon"), and some of the rooms are positioned at angles that result in odd corners and closets that go into other closets. Tunnels at the rear of the house are supposed to have led to the White House and to the Potomac River.

Legend has it that some enemies of President Lincoln once planned to abduct him and spirit him from the White House via the tunnel system of the deserted Octagon. Their plan was to have a boat waiting for them at the river. It is just one of many stories that sprang up during the time the house was empty after the Tayloe family no longer lived there.

Except for the period during the War of 1812, the Tayloe family occupied the Octagon from the time it was completed in the early 1800's until Mrs. Tayloe's death in 1855. The Colonel and his wife had fifteen children, seven sons and eight daughters. One article from a nineteenth century newspaper said that the Tayloe girls were as famed for their grace, charm, and beauty as for their wealth.

The Octagon, one of Washington's oldest houses, was visited by all the leading figures of the new government, some of whom still drop by from time to time.

136 According to the stories that have survived, some of their love affairs were turbulent and involved dramatic denouements on the huge oval staircase. A striking bell lantern hung down the stairwell from a twenty-two-foot chain and cast a shadowy light on the large statues that occupied niches in the wall of the main stairs, giving the entry hall an ominous air that set the stage for the arguments and violence that are a part of the Octagon's history.

Early in the 1800's, one of the Tayloe girls was supposed to have fallen in love with a British officer, but feelings between the United States and Great Britain were so hostile that her father would have no part of such a relationship. His refusal to allow the Englishman to set foot in his house sparked several loud arguments. It was just after one of these heated battles on a dark and stormy night that the girl grabbed up her candle and stomped up the stairs. As she neared the top, there was a scream and her body plunged down the stairwell and landed in a crumpled heap beneath the swaying bell lantern. One reporter recalling the story decades later, quoted some who speculated that the clash with her father proved too much and she chose to end her life, and others who theorized that she tripped and fell over the railing.

This daughter's restless spirit is said to still haunt that stairway on certain stormy nights. A flickering candle may be seen casting the shadows of the railing against the opposite wall as it moves upward one step at a time. According to those who have witnessed it, the drama always ends the same way. There is a shriek, followed a second later by a sickening thud.

The death of his daughter grieved the Colonel and further hardened his feelings toward the British. Storytellers also say that he was haunted by the spirit of his departed daughter and sought to stay away from the house of her death. When the War of 1812 erupted, he reasoned

The spirits of the Tayloe sisters have been seen re-enacting their tragic deaths on this stairway, and the hanging lantern at times swaying for no discernible reason.

that flight to his Mount Airy plantation would offer him the escape from her presence and from the British he so hated. Using the excuse that he feared harm might come to his family if they remained in Washington, Tayloe arranged with the French Ambassador to the United States to make the Octagon his official residence, and left for North Carolina.

Many historians say that had it not been for the French flag flying over the Octagon when the British put torches to Washington, the house would have gone up in flames. The British had overrun the Americans at Bladensburg and moved into the city with little resistance. Few buildings escaped their torches, including the President's House.

When Colonel Tayloe heard of the plight of the President, he wrote to Madison at his Virginia home offering the Octagon as a temporary home while 1600 Pennsylvania Avenue was being rebuilt. Eager to return to Washington, the Madisons accepted the generous offer and moved into the Octagon during the fall of 1814. The Madisons kept up a round of Washington social functions and tried to bolster the spirits of the war-weary citizens. The war was not a popular one, and the charred ruins in the city made the dark cloud hanging over Washington even darker. It was five months after the Madisons had moved into the Octagon that a courier from Ghent brought the President the treaty that had declared the end of the war the previous December. Madison ratified the treaty in a room at the head of the stairs on the second floor of the Octagon.

The parties at the Octagon began in earnest. The first was an informal open house, but after that the guest lists for the celebrations included foreign diplomats, congressmen, local politicians, military leaders, and the cream of the Federal City's society.

If anyone in Washington knew how to celebrate the end of a war, it was Dolley Madison. Well known for her social grace, she generally greeted her guests dressed in the latest fashions topped by a plumed turban that made her appear taller. She was quite conscious about her shortness.

President James Madison and his wife, Dolley, lived in the Octagon while the White House was being rebuilt after the British put the torch to it. Dolley loved the Octagon so much that her spirit is said to visit from time to time manifested as a cold spot scented with the fragrance of lilacs, the scent she almost always wore.

Parties were an almost daily affair at the Octagon while the Madisons lived there. They seemed to be equally relaxed entertaining forty or so friends, or four hundred or more guests.

Years after the Madison era, in the second half of the nineteenth century, newspapers were writing accounts about apparitions of footmen dressed in the full uniform of that period, hailing the carriages of guests. They quoted some who said that they had heard the sounds of wheels rumbling over gravel roads, the opening and closing of carriage doors, and the fading sounds of carriages rolling away.

This was just one of several phenomena associated with the Octagon that the press has chronicled. Dolley Madison's spirit has been seen standing in front of the mantelpiece in the ballroom, where she used to receive her guests over a century and a half ago. One article described "the wispy form of the turbaned hostess," who was seen dancing through the entrance hall.

Some say that it was during one of Dolley's lavish parties that she slipped away for a rendezvous in the garden with Aaron Burr. Burr is supposed to have scaled a ten-foot wall just to see the President's wife. Apparently it was a "welcome back" encounter. Burr had spent several years in European exile, following his controversial duel with Alexander Hamilton. Burr had been Dolley Payne Todd's suitor before she accepted James Madison.

The President's House was rebuilt, and the Madisons returned to 1600 Pennsylvania Avenue, where they remained until the end of Madison's second term. Meanwhile, with the threat of danger removed, the Tayloes returned to Washington. However, the family was to experience more tragedy in that home.

One of the Tayloe daughters, who had eloped against the wishes of her father, had returned to beg his forgiveness. Legend has it that they met on the stairway. The Colonel couldn't bring himself to forgive his daughter for not marrying the gentleman of position he had chosen for her. The Colonel, in an ill-tempered mood, hardly glanced at his young daughter as he continued down the stairs.

The smell of food cooking sometimes drifts from the kitchen in the basement of the Octagon. When the source of the odors is investigated, however, the room is always deserted.

The girl was in his path, and not wishing to continue the discussion, he tried to push her aside. The girl either lost her balance or fell trying to escape her father's touch. She tumbled past the Colonel and fell dead of a broken neck at the foot of the stairs.

It is difficult to imagine what must have gone through the Colonel's mind as he saw a second daughter become a victim of that stairway. Some think that the shock of losing two of his girls on that ominous oval stairway contributed, in part, to his own death at the relatively young age of fifty-seven.

The spirit of the second Tayloe girl who met death on that stairway continues to return to the scene of the accident. Some people who have never heard the tale walk around the spot at the foot of the stairs where the young girl's body once lay in a crumpled mass. Perhaps they sense a cold spot or pick up other vibrations.

According to the legend of the house, other dramas that have unfolded here are also replayed. For more than a hundred years, Octagon residents were plagued by thumping sounds from within the walls. Try as they would, no one was able to track down the source. Then one day as workmen were repairing a wall they came upon the skeleton of a young girl. The finger bones on both hands were clenched tight, as though she had died knocking on the wall. Her skeleton was taken out of the wall and given a proper burial. The thumping sounds were never again heard in that part of the house.

At the time, one of the Colonel's descendants said that she seemed to recall a tale her grandmother had told of a British soldier and a slave girl when the French embassy was at the Octagon back in 1814. They were lovers, but in a jealous rage, the soldier killed her and somehow managed to seal her body inside a hollow wall.

After the death of Mrs. John Tayloe in 1855, the mansion changed hands several times and was allowed to deteriorate. The constant acting out of its violent history during late night hours was enough to keep most people away.

Sometime after the Tayloes moved out and before the outbreak of the Civil War, an old gambler and his retinue of women occupied the upper floors of the decaying old mansion. It was a more than suitable place for the activities of the gambler. He became fascinated by the intricately designed bellpull system used to summon servants, and used to position himself at his card table so that he was within reach of the rope by which he was constantly summoning food or drink or one of his female cohorts.

One night the gambler was assaulted by a hard-drinking farmer he had cheated. As the farmer knocked the gambler across the room, the gambler supposedly grabbed the bellpull for support while he reached for his gun. The farmer's gun exploded first and the gambler crumpled to the floor frantically clutching the bellpull. There have been various letters and articles written down through the years that indicate the gambler, whose ghost is one of those that frequent the Octagon, has often grabbed for it since that night. It is said that he returns again and clutches the bellpull, still hoping that he will get to his gun in time.

Reporters have frequently filed stories about tales of screams of agony and sobs and moans of despair echoing through the Octagon. Before the turn of the last century, one writer said, "The spectral goings on there are so extraordinary that no one will live in the house." The article attributed the moans and sobs to a slave who had been whipped or otherwise tortured to death by "the former proprietor of the establishment." Other articles have offered different explanations. One reporter said that sometime after the Tayloes had lived in the house, its river tunnel had been used as a link to the Underground Railroad. During the Civil War, the Union Army had used the house as a war records office, and temporarily as a place of care and treatment for wounded and dying men. The sounds of sobbing and moaning could be from the souls of runaway slaves crying out in nightmares of previously endured tortures, or the agony of men wounded in battle.

On April 18, 1891, a story in the *Washington Star* told about how the Sis-

Colonel John Tayloe, who built the Octagon, couldn't bear to live there after tragic accidents claimed two of his daughters. Some say their dying screams haunted him and kept him from sleeping.

ters of Charity moved into the house "after purifying it from top to bottom with holy water." It didn't work. When the Sisters of Charity fell victim to the bizarre goings on and had to move, it was time for something to be done. Another newspaper article told of how a dozen men took it upon themselves to investigate. Determined to put the ghost talk to rest once and for all, the men gathered up their sleeping bags and went inside the Octagon to spend the night. They vowed to capture anyone responsible for generating the "ghosts."

Shortly after midnight, a reporter said, "female shrieks, the clanking of sabers, and thumping sounds in the wall" drove the twelve men to seek slumber elsewhere.

In 1902 the American Institute of Architects acquired the Octagon. Less than a score of years ago, a caretaker told a newspaper reporter how he returned after a night out with his family to find all of the lights on. The house was locked up tight, just as he had left it. Everything inside seemed normal. However, the edge of the carpet at the foot of the stairs was turned over—right at the very spot where death had claimed one of the Tayloe girls.

Many who visit the three-story brick structure have claimed that it is not uncommon to encounter the aroma of food being prepared in the kitchen. When they investigate, they find the kitchen deserted and the food there made of wax.

In the 1950's, a doctor who had made a house call at the Octagon had a strange encounter on the stairway. Caretaker James Cyprus had summoned the physician for his ailing wife. The doctor was preparing to leave when he mustered up enough courage to ask Cyprus if there was a costume party going on that evening.

"No, there isn't," Cyprus replied. The doctor looked perplexed and told him of encountering a man on the stairs just a few moments before who had been dressed in a military uniform of the early 1800's. The doctor told Cyprus he had had to move over to let the man pass.

John Sherwood described that incident in the *Washington Star* in August of 1965. He also wrote that "Velma May, curator of the house, has seen the big chandelier that hangs down the stairwell swing of its own volition. Another time she found tiptoeing tracks of human feet in the undisturbed dust on the top floor landing."

Even quite recently there have been reports of encounters with Dolley Madison's spirit, which often manifests itself surrounded by the fragrance of lilacs. Apparently she still visits often, for I have had several encounters related to me. One report was from an official with the American Institute of Architects. He did not want to be identified, but he said that on two separate occasions when he was showing people through the house during its renovation in the 1960's, they had mentioned walking through a pocket of scented air.

In neither case was the party who made contact aware of the legends. The AIA official swore that no flowers were in bloom. In fact, he said that he stood within a few feet of the person in the pocket of perfume and he couldn't get a whiff. On another occasion a person walked into such a pocket, walked out of it, and then stepped back into it.

An assistant secretary for the Institute related a few years ago how she had sensed the presence of someone with her in one of the Octagon rooms. The woman told of hearing a very deep "sigh" while waiting for someone to come down from the third floor, which has now been converted to offices. She didn't think too much about the sound but was surprised to turn around after hearing it again to find no one there. The presence she felt made her ill at ease. She never put the experience out of her mind, especially after learning that the room she had been waiting in had been used by Dolley Madison as a bedroom.

When the American Institute of Architects was preparing for the Octagon restoration, an architectural photographer was commissioned to provide material for the renovation committee. He took interior and exterior photographs, and the AIA had them processed. One picture turned out to be highly unusual. Without knowing it, the photographer had caught on film the apparition of a woman slipping into the house from the rear garden. She was passing through the locked rear doors. The AIA official who told me the story said the form wasn't clear enough to determine whether it was Dolley Madison. "Of course," he said, "It could also have been one of the Tayloes."

When I first visited the Octagon in 1970, the curator, who had been there for about six months, was reluctant to discuss the old tales. The house was just being reopened to the public after extensive restoration work, and she said that the Octagon board of directors was more interested in publicity about the historical significance of the house. She confessed a personal interest, even an inquisitiveness, about the ghost stories but steadfastly maintained that since she had been there, she had neither seen nor heard anything unusual.

"Yes," she said, "the floors creak very nicely. Some of the doors also have squeaks." She rightly insisted that that

There was a time when sounds of gaiety were heard in the mansion of General John Peter Van Ness. Even after the house was vacant, sounds were heard, not all of them happy.

wasn't evidence of ghosts. She also related how she had often worked late into the evening but had encountered no apparitions or supernatural phenomena of any sort.

In December of 1972, I had occasion to return to the Octagon on another assignment. As I sat by the curator's desk, the phone rang. It was her husband, apparently telling her he would be working late. As she discussed other methods of transportation home, I heard her say, "You know I don't really care to stay in this house alone after dark."

The curator wouldn't discuss that remark with me and seemed edgy. I soon left, but I couldn't help but wonder what caused such a change in so short a time. Within a few months the Octagon had another curator.

GENERAL VAN NESS'S HEADLESS HORSES

Thousands of Washingtonians and tourists alike pass by the Pan American Union Building at 17th and Constitution daily, yet few are familiar with the mansion that occupied the land for almost one hundred years. Fewer still are familiar with the legends associated with it during the last quarter century of its existence.

They called it the Van Ness mansion, after the man who ordered it built back in 1816. John Peter Van Ness was a well-liked New York politician and a protégé of Aaron Burr—the newly elected Vice President—who came south to the Sixth Congress. He met Marcia Burns, daughter of the man who sold the government much of the land on which the Federal City is built, and decided to adopt Washington as his home. That didn't go well with his New York constituents, who voted him out of office in 1803. For a few years, Van Ness and his wife lived with his father-in-law, David Burns, in an old log house that the wealthy Burns's family called home.

Van Ness had many influential friends and no one enjoyed politics or entertain-

The ghost of Marcia Van Ness, who sought consolation by helping orphans when her only child died in childbirth, is said to have haunted the Van Ness mansion after her death.

General John Peter Van Ness, one-time mayor of Washington, whose mansion rivaled the White House in design and beauty.

ing more than he did. He contented himself with entertaining and with managing his wife's estate. When Van Ness decided to build his own house, Benjamin Latrobe was the only man capable of designing a suitable setting for the type of entertaining Van Ness had in mind. Newspaper articles written about the mansion say that few homes in any city could rival it. It was supposed to have been the first house in America to have indoor plumbing that supplied hot and cold running water. Another reporter described it as "the city's finest" home, and remarked that the cream of Washington society visited there often. The north portico of the house was modeled after the White House, right down to the same number of pillars. The south front faced the river, and looked out on an immense fruit orchard, according to an article in *Washingtonia, The Nation's Weekly,* July 16, 1910.

The house was completed a few years after the War of 1812 had ended, and most of Washington was still in a festive mood. Among those popular on the so-cial circuit were Stephen and Susan Decatur, and John Quincy Adams. In the following years John Van Ness entertained most of the city's elite—including John C. Calhoun, Attorney General William Wirt, Henry Clay, and others from the legislative, judicial, and executive branches of government. Van Ness had wanted the house finished by the time his only daughter, Ann, returned from school in Philadelphia, so that she would have a suitable place to entertain young gentleman callers. It wasn't long before Ann Van Ness married Arthur Middleton of South Carolina, son of one of the signers of the Declaration of Independence. Van Ness was heartbroken when Ann died in childbirth in 1822. The baby was stillborn.

He managed to overcome his sadness by plunging himself deeper into his work. (He had become mayor of Washington and also was a general in the Militia.) One writer said that deeply religious Marcia Van Ness found solace in her charitable activities for a while, but her grief manifested itself in failing health, and within a few years she died. Newspapers of the day said that she was given a public funeral, apparently the first woman in the United States to be so honored, and that children from the orphan asylum walked beside her bier.

It was difficult for a man like Van Ness to survive the loss of his family. He pulled himself together by vowing that his wife, his departed daughter, and the grandchild he had never gotten to know would have a final resting place befitting his love for them. One reporter said that he personally supervised construction of the mausoleum, which was of the finest brick and marble and cost $30,000, about half the cost of his mansion. Another reporter described it as "an exact replica of the pillared temple of Tivoli." The mausoleum sits atop the highest hill in Oak Hill Cemetery looking down on picturesque Rock Creek.

Having provided his family with an eternal resting place, Van Ness began to increase his activities once again, though some who knew him well said at the time that it was obvious the sparkle had gone from his personality. Van Ness had almost become a legend in his lifetime. For years newspapers recorded no larger banquets for the members of Congress than the annual affairs at his home. As his age advanced, his body grew weaker and his mind returned more and more frequently to the days he had had with his wife, and the days he had not had with his grandchild.

An increasingly despondent Van Ness began to withdraw into the shadows of his home, not only losing contact with his friends, but with reality as well. Reports from the period say that he didn't care that the mansion was decaying and his staff dwindling. Whispers circulated about certain rooms in the old mansion that no one entered, and that more than one spirit roamed the corridors. Allegedly, laughter from his departed daughter evaporated into bloodcurdling screams, similar to those she had made just before dying in childbirth. One article mentioned "footsteps unattached to human bodies"; another brief story focused on a small lady "in quaint costume and wearing an old-fashioned bonnet," who had been seen wandering the hallways upstairs.

Van Ness was pictured as having been so caught up in his despair that he paid the tales little, if any, attention. Even when the household staff began to leave, he made no effort to replace them, hastening the decay of the house, in which he died in 1846.

When death called John Peter Van Ness to join his family, his body was placed on a bier that was pulled to Oak Hill Cemetery by his six most cherished white horses. The United States was at war with Mexico, and yet Washington took time to mourn a man who had been loved by many. One writer recalled that "many private houses on the route of the funeral procession were draped in mourning."

During the graveside ceremony high on Oak Hill, the white stallions were observed munching grass by the mausoleum. When they lowered their heads behind a mound, one mourner sobbed, "They've buried their heads with their master." In a few days most of the mourners put John Van Ness out of their minds and resumed the routines of the living. However, for some others it wasn't that simple. His decaying mansion was a reminder to them of his happier years. They wanted it restored as a memorial to the man. The opposition believed it could produce only nightmares, for ghostly tales had increased since the funeral, and now included new and strange reports of activity on the mansion grounds.

In the early part of this century, one writer interviewed some of those who had experienced supernatural manifestations associated with the Van Ness mansion. Some who had dared to stroll the deserted, expansive grounds during the late night hours, were quoted as saying that they had heard sounds of laughter and gaiety float from the old house, as though still carried on the winds that swept through the once beautifully manicured trees. In the 1920's a writer recalled an incident that had happened to the wife of a caretaker. The woman swore that a wispy woman appeared before her bedside late one night and attempted to give her a message to relay to someone in another part of the city. The message was lost, however, because the woman's husband awakened and rolled over, and the spirit vanished.

Other witnesses have been quoted as having said that they had seen the specters of six headless white horses gallop-

ing around the mansion grounds. One witness told a reporter that the moonlight was "so bright their gleaming coats looked like silver." Stories about the six headless white horses have persisted down through the years, even though the mansion of John Peter Van Ness was torn down in 1903. More than half a century later, one newspaper article retold the legend, declaring that the phantom horses are almost always spotted on the anniversary of the General's death, retracing that journey to Oak Hill Cemetery and circling the grounds of the Pan American Union Building at a gallop—frantically searching for their master.

Just a few years ago a motorist tried to explain to police that he had run his car off Rock Creek Parkway because he had seen the shimmering forms of six headless white horses up by the Van Ness mausoleum. His excuse may have kept the legend alive, but it did nothing for the man's reputation for being able to hold his liquor.

THE KALORAMA LEGACY

There was a time when a large expanse of Northwest Washington was occupied by the Kalorama estate of Joel Barlow. The manor house was constructed in 1807 and stood on what is now the 2300 block of S Street, Northwest. It is said that one could look over the rolling countryside from the manor house and see both Rock Creek and the Potomac. Inventor Robert Fulton used to test some of his boats in the waters below Kalorama.

In the early 1800's, Kalorama was the home of General John Bomford, a close friend of Stephen Decatur and his wife, Susan. When the Commodore was killed, Susan Decatur became a guest of the Bomfords' for quite some time. Apparently she was very ill at ease at the home

The six white horses that pulled the coffin of John Van Ness to Oak Hill Cemetery have been spotted circling the family mausoleum.

she had once shared with her husband on the President's Square. The General allowed Decatur to be buried in the tomb on the Kalorama estate.

There is a legend that Decatur's spirit was unhappy at Kalorama and blood from his wound would appear periodically on the outside of the tomb. Some say that's why Susan Decatur finally ordered the body removed to Philadelphia where his parents were buried, hoping that a final resting place there would stop the crimson stain from appearing.

During the Civil War, Kalorama became a hospital for wounded and dying soldiers. Hundreds of them were cared for on the grounds of the mansion, and the first tales of supernatural events associated with the house date from this period.

On Christmas eve of 1865, the troops at Kalorama Hospital decided to throw a party. It was a festive occasion, but for some it would be their last. Reporters quoted fire officials who said that a defective stovepipe turned the evening into a nightmare. The fire spread through the entire east wing of the structure before it was brought under control.

By dawn looters had replaced the fire fighters but they were dispersed, and though the old hospital was severely damaged, much of it was saved. It wasn't long, however, before tales began to spring up about the old Kalorama ruins and the tree-shaded grounds. People began taking a different path in order to avoid "sinister shadows." One article I read said that the building never lost the damp and musty odor it acquired after the fire. Cries of anguish are said to have shattered the calmness of many a night on that hillside above Rock Creek.

Some of the visitors to the old hospital ruins have told reporters of hearing the "rustling of silks and satins" from an earlier and happier period of the house's history. Others swore to having seen the shapes of "handsome men and elegant ladies" adorning the halls and rooms that were lighted only by the moon shining through the burned-out roof.

But reports of moans and groans have been more prominent over the years. An article in the *Washington Star* in June of 1905 devoted considerable attention to the sounds of Kalorama. "The few people who lived in the vicinity were seized with cold tremors when they heard the howls and screeches that came from within the walls." The reporter described these sounds as "enough to freeze the marrow in one's bones."

Occasionally, a visitor to Kalorama would report "a chill-of-the-spine" accompanied by "goosebumps on the flesh" as he entered one of the many cold spots in the old house. Indeed, several area residents, who often braved the early evening darkness to stroll over the remains of the Kalorama estate, said that they encountered what appeared to be "moving" or "roaming" cold spots. Some of these were described as carrying with them the stench of morphine, blood, sweat, and gunpowder.

Washington's burgeoning population quickly encroached on the Kalorama estate. The grounds became smaller and smaller, as the city's quarter of a million people pushed outward. In the last decade of the 1800's, Kalorama itself—or what was left ot it—was replaced by a new home. All traces of that earlier Washington era were wiped away. Well, almost all traces. Authorities on the history of Kalorama say the estate may be gone, but cold spots that are permeated with a sickly smell still persist in several places on its site, and they believe that a few former Kalorama residents still drop by the neighborhood from time to time.

THE INCONSOLABLE SPIRIT OF WOODROW WILSON

It has been half a century since President Woodrow Wilson died, yet according to some Washingtonians he still visits his old home in Northwest Washington.

Wilson began his physical decline in the fall of 1919 after suffering a stroke. However, his wife, Edith, and those close to him shielded him from the public, keeping his disability a secret. When he left office in 1921, President Wilson and his wife moved into an elegant house just

off Embassy Row, at 2340 S Street, Northwest.

Looking old, worn, and haggard, Wilson the citizen lived out the remainder of his years in a quiet routine at his new home. He moved about with an ever-present cane from the large collection he owned. An elevator helped him get upstairs to the bedroom.

Wilson never quite recovered from the country's rejection of his dream—the League of Nations. Some newspaper accounts from that era indicate that he brooded. Sources close to him were quoted as saying that he had periodic lapses of memory and what still other friends described as "unpredictable crying spells."

Woodrow Wilson died about three years after leaving office, but several old-timers say that he hasn't left his beloved home. Legend has it that the former President has been heard more than once climbing the stairs to his bedroom.

Woodrow Wilson in happier days before he retired to the house on S Street, Northwest, where he lived out his last years.

Some who used to work in the home have sworn to hearing sounds that remind them of a man sobbing, and they speculate that it's Wilson's spirit still unable to cope with the shattering of his dream for the League of Nations.

An article in the *Washington Post* in 1969 focused on a caretaker at the Wilson house who had had enough of the "slow shuffle." He told the reporter that it sounded like someone walking with a cane. I talked with a carpenter and a gardener who also indicated that they had heard some strange noises in the house when they had been around late. However, the hostesses who now man the house for the National Trust for Historic Preservation, insist that the sounds are caused by an aging house, not the ghost of a former President.

INDEX

Nixon, Tricia, *see* Cox, Tricia Nixon

Octagon House, The, 35, 133–42, **134–35**
  kitchen, **139**
  stairwell, **136–37**
"Old Brick Capitol," 85–90, **86–87,** 116
"Old Howard," 98–99
"Old Man Eloquent," *see* Adams, John Quincy
O'Neil, Peggy, *see* Eaton, Peggy O'Neil

Paine, *see* Powell, Louis
Pan American Union Building, site of, 142, 145
Parapsychological phenomena, *see* supernatural phenomena
Parks, Lillian Rogers, 56
Payne, Dorothea ("Dolley"), *see* Madison, Dorothea Payne
"Peace of God" monument, *see* "Grief"
Penrose, Boise, Senator, 79
Pension Building, 103–07, **102–03, 106**
Poltergeist, 98, 121, *see also* supernatural phenomena
Post Office Department, The, 41, 94
Potomac River, 8–11, *see also* Three Sisters' Curse
Powell, Louis (Paine), 45
Presidents, U.S., *see individual entries*
"President's House ," *see* White House
"President's Square," *see* Lafayette Square
Prominent American Ghosts, 61

Quarters A, U.S. Navy Yard, *see* Tingey House

Randolph, John, Congressman, 41
Rathbone, Claire (Clara) Harris, 47, **48**
Rathbone, Henry, Major, 47–48, **47**
Reed, Dr. Walter, 115, **119**
Reynolds, Evalyn McLean, **130–31**
Reynolds, Robert Rice, Senator, 130
Roosevelt, Eleanor
  White House ghosts mentioned by, 64
Roosevelt, Theodore, President
  Lincoln's ghost observed by, 63
Robb, Lynda Johnson
  White House ghosts mentioned by, 60

Saint-Gaudens, Augustus
  sculptor of "Grief," 48–49
St. John's Church, Lafayette Square, 33–35, **34**
Sandburg, Carl
  Lincoln's ghost mentioned by, 59
Seward, Frederick, 45
Seward, William, Secretary of State, 45–46, **46**
Seward House (Old Washington Club), 45–46
Sherburne, John, 111, *see also* duels
Sherman, Anthony, aide to Washington, 109
Shockle, Charles (medium), 61
Sickles, Daniel, Congressman, **42,** 42–43, **43,** 44–45, **44**
  severed leg of, *see* Medical Museum
Sickles, Theresa, **42,** 42–44
Simms, "Bishop" (barber)
  ghost of, 77
Sinclair, Harry, 130, *see also* Harding, Warren G.
Sisters of Charity, at Octagon House, 140
Sixth Street and Pennsylvania Avenue, N.W.

Hotel, visited by ghost, 120
Skeletons, 122, 139
Slaves, *see* Underground Railroad
Smith, John, Captain
  diary, 7, *see* Three Sisters' Curse
Spiritualism, 2, 63
Spiritualist Church, First, 90
States rights, ghostly debate over, 40
Stoddert, Benjamin, Secretary of Navy, **13,** 35, *see also* Halcyon House
  chair of, **23**
Supernatural phenomena, *see also* Ghosts, Haunted Houses
Supernatural phenomena
  blood stains, 26–27, 78, 146
  candle flickering, 136
  curtains fluttering, 20
  lantern swaying, 136
  levitation incidents, 20–22, 61
  lightning, 10–11
  lights turned on and off, 22, 24, 27, 140–41
  objects, displayed
    coffin, 114
    doors, ripped from hinges, 102
    iron bar lifted, 120
    locked window opened, 120
    blankets removed, 121
  shadows, 146
Supernatural phenomena, auditory
  banging shutters, 120
  clanking sabers, 140
  clucking, 72
  coughing and sneezing, 77
  cries of anguish, 146
  doors squeaking, 26
  drum rolls, 30
  floors creaking, 26
  footsteps, 16, 20, 21, 24, 76, 97, 144, 147
  howls and screeches, 146
  laughter, 56, 89, 114
  marching troops, 11–12
  moans and groans, 7, 15–16, 26, 48, 49, 111, 140, 146
  music, 90
  opening and closing doors, 120
  rap, of gavel, 74
  rapping and tapping, 13, 16, 24, 30, 61, 99
  rocking (chair), 121
  rustling, 97, 146
  screams and shrieks, 15, 136, 140, 144
  sighs, 141
  singing, 77
  sobs, 15–16, 26, 48, 49, 111, 140, 147
  squeaks, 114
  stomping, 121
  swishing sounds, 28
  thud, 136
  thumping sounds, 139, 140
  thunder, 10, 30
  voices, 19, 41, 59
  wind, gusts of, 16
Supernatural phenomena, olfactory
  aroma of food cooking, 139, 141
  odor "of charnel house," 114
  fragrance of lilacs, 138, 141
  scent of soap, 78, 54
  stench of battlefield, 146
Supernatural phenomena, sensations